THE SILVER LINK LIBRARY OF RAILWAY MODELLING

•

LOCOMOTIVE AND ROLLING-STOCK CONSTRUCTION

THE SILVER LINK LIBRARY OF RAILWAY MODELLING

•

LOCOMOTIVE AND ROLLING-STOCK CONSTRUCTION

Choosing suitable stock * Building kits
* Painting and detailing * Realistic operation

•

A series of books providing a no-nonsense
step-by-step guide to model railway construction

Trevor Booth

Silver Link Publishing Ltd

In this volume the products of certain manufacturers have been used as examples, and the manufacturers have been clearly identified. The author has no commercial connections with these manufacturers, and their products have been selected as being either the most appropriate models for the layout and/or models that show as many different designs and materials as possible.

First published in August 1995

British Library Cataloguing in Publication Data

A catalogue record for this book is available from the British Library.

ISBN 1 85794 038 5

Silver Link Publishing Ltd
Unit 5
Home Farm Close
Church Street
Wadenhoe
Peterborough PE8 5TE
Tel/fax (01832) 720440

Printed and bound in Great Britain

ACKNOWLEDGEMENTS

Grateful thanks are due to David Hampson for allowing me access to and use of his photographic collection. Similarly to Bob Essery, John Robinson, Barry Lane and John Matthews of the LMS Society for photographs and helpful advice on all matters LMS; also to Ian Tattersall for LNWR information.

To Bob Lomax and John Wallwork, for providing me with locomotives to photograph, and, in Bob's case, for carrying out some of the construction. Special thanks to my wife Susan for typing the manuscript and putting up with a railway modeller!

BIBLIOGRAPHY

Dow, George *Midland Carriages* (Wild Swan)
Jenkinson, David, and Essery, Bob An Illustrated History of LMS Locomotives (Vols 1 and 2 OPC; Vols 3, 4 and 5 Silver Link Publishing Ltd)
An Illustrated History of LMS Coaches (OPC 1977)
Jenkinson, David, and Campling, N. *Historic Carriage Drawings in 4mm Scale* (Ian Allan 1969)

Rowland, Don *British Railways Wagons* (David & Charles 1985)
Various authors: 'British Railways Past and Present' series, various area and county volumes (Past and Present Publishing Ltd)

CONTENTS

INTRODUCTION

This, the third in the series of model railway construction books in the Silver Link Library of Railway Modelling, deals essentially with choosing the most appropriate locomotives, carriages and wagons for your model railway, their use and, of course, the detailed construction of the models. There is also mention of operation and running the layout.

As with the previous two volumes, we have tried to range far and wide in the coverage of the techniques, materials and philosophy in building up this most fascinating of all aspects of railway modelling. The core of the detailed construction is the material used for the Platt Lane project layout, and in choosing the models built for it we have adopted the approach suggested before, that of looking to the real thing for inspiration rather than guessing. Looking to reality enables us to get a feel for what looks right on the model, and I firmly believe, that in doing so the model railway builder will ultimately gain more satisfaction from the model he or she creates.

The approach to railway modelling outlined in this series has been one of trying to create image and atmosphere, elusive rather than concrete concepts I appreciate, but concepts that add more to a model railway than strict dimensional accuracy. In the earlier volumes this was likened to the approach of an Impressionist painter - looking at the total picture rather than concentrating too much on individual elements.

The same approach has been adopted with the locomotives and rolling-stock. There are no excuses for using inappropriate locos, or having models of a pristine quality that would immediately alienate them from the rest of the layout. It is therefore hoped that in this volume you will be encouraged to look carefully at your choice of locomotives and rolling-stock and be encouraged similarly to consider their most appropriate usage.

I should also mention that I have been railway

modelling now for the best part of 20 years, and during that time I have become familiar with much of the terminology or jargon used both by modellers and the railways themselves. It is therefore easy for me to assume, perhaps incorrectly, that readers will also be familiar with this. Realising that this may not be the case, I have included a glossary of terms, and the sections on basic modelling techniques such as soldering and painting will also help to redress this.

During my modelling I have developed not only the approach described in this series of books but also my own methods of achieving it. You might not agree with them and may well have developed your own techniques - it is inevitable that as you gain experience you will develop your own methods. Those outlined have worked for me, but they are examples, not tablets of stone.

Railway modelling is a hobby, intended for relaxation, and while the approaches taken might not suit everyone, I hope they will at least provide some food for thought, and that if you are tempted to follow the thinking behind the project model, you will find that it adds a little more to the complete picture, helping to establish that all-too-elusive *atmosphere*.

Addresses of manufacturers and suppliers

Chowbent Castings, 325 North Road, Atherton, Manchester M29 0RF

DJH, Leadgate Industrial Estate, Consett, County Durham DH8 7RS

Alan Gibson, The Bungalow, Church Road, Lingwood, Norwich, Norfolk NR13 4TR

Home of O Gauge, 528 Kingston Road, Raynes Park, London SW20

Parkside Dundas, Millie Street, Kirkcaldy, Fife KY1 2NL

Slaters Plasticard, Temple Road, Matlock Bath, Matlock, Derbys DE4 3PG

Wigan Wagon Works, 3 Gidlow Avenue, Wigan WN6 7PF

1.
SERVICES TO PLATT LANE

This series of books is aimed at showing how a model railway can be developed with illustrations and practical applications of the techniques used on the Platt Lane project layout. I thought, therefore, that it might be useful at the outset to recap briefly on what has happened so far.

The story so far

The approach taken with Platt Lane has been to show how much more effective a model railway can be if it is related to reality - real railway practice and a real landscape, whether it be the Great Northern or the Union Pacific.

I have adopted a 'holistic' approach, not relying only on my favourite aspects or interests and allowing them to dominate the model railway, but regarding the model as a whole and concentrating on trying to create the *whole* picture rather than a series of detail items. I am seeking that all-too-elusive atmosphere of a *real* railway.

Just as Platt Lane, or indeed any other model railway, to be effective draws on reality for the buildings and trackwork, for example, reality must also be drawn on for the locomotives and rolling-stock, be it a bucolic branch line or an industrial layout.

No matter how much care and effort is spent in creating the layout, the whole image can be spoiled by the simple expedient of using inappropriate locomotives, rolling-stock and train formations and movements. For example, there is the passenger train that barely stops at the platform before accelerating out with the sort of speed ratio more akin to a Space Shuttle than a railway train; or the minimalist goods yard favoured by the branch-line modeller hosting not general merchandise wagons but specialist vehicles such as gunpowder or iron ore wagons; or, perhaps

Here, well illustrated, is a point made in the text. For safety and operational reasons the railways operated by rules that expressly covered the marshalling of trains and other formations. This '4F' is hauling a train in which there is, as required, space between the loco and the tank wagons, in this case provided by two open wagons. Other rules concerned the placing of loaded cattle and livestock vehicles immediately behind the loco (this didn't apply when they were empty) and the placing of fitted vehicles together at the front when the train is composed of both fitted and unfitted vehicles. On the LMS this latter type of train was referred to as a 'Maltese' freight because of the symbol used to denote it in the working timetable. *D. Hampson*

rather more subtle but equally part of the picture, the steam-hauled train of petrol tankers with no buffing or packing wagons between the loco and the tank wagons.

There are, as I think has been acknowledged throughout this series, limitations as to what can be achieved on a model, but to whatever standard you model, whatever your particular interests in a model railway or whatever scale, gauge, period or country you model, it will look and feel a lot better in operation and give more satisfaction if it has more of a resemblance to reality than the fertility of imagination! But put the two together by adapting reality *imaginatively*, and you might just be on the way to a more satisfying model railway.

Historical background

A useful point at which to start looking at the operation of railways and the appropriate locomotives and vehicles used to service their operational requirements might well be the development and practices of the railways themselves - in the case of Platt Lane, the railways of Britain.

The development of the railway system in Britain was largely haphazard, based on countless Acts of Parliament that promoted countless small and some not-so-small railways, some of which never actually got beyond the dreams of their promoters. This led to much duplication of routes, to rival companies building rural lines competing for the same routes and traffic, and to some lines being strongly promoted locally and actually built, but which, rationally, should not have been.

In France, by contrast, though the railways were not nationalised until 1939, there was from the early days much more of a planned approach, which avoided the duplication seen in this country; the state planned the main-line systems and owned the track and routes, and leased them to the railway companies. There was also a state railway company, the ETAT, which operated effectively a 'region' of the main system.

The duplication and rivalry in the UK did, however, lead to some very interesting lines, such as the Settle & Carlisle, and practices that lasted well into the 1960s but which had their origins in those early days; because they influenced much of what was to happen on British Railways until the Beeching era, they therefore provide much of interest for the railway modeller.

If, for example, we look at the inspiration for our project layout, Great Moor Street in Bolton, we find that it was an London & North Western Railway incursion into the very heart of the Lancashire & Yorkshire Railway, not more than a few miles from the latter's Horwich locomotive works and yards from the L&Y's expansive and comprehensive Trinity Street station, which had direct

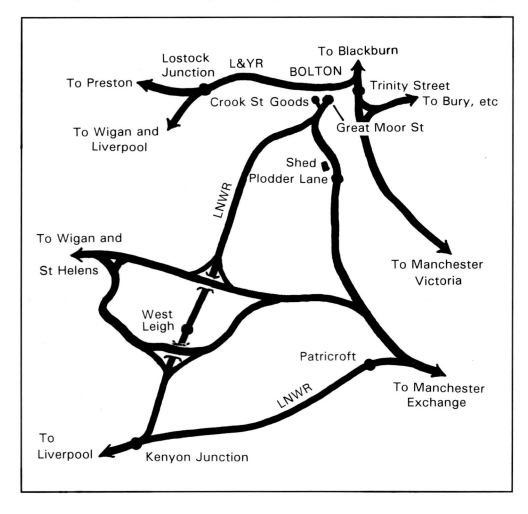

Sketch map of LNWR and L&YR lines around Bolton.

links to east Lancashire, Manchester, Yorkshire, Liverpool, Preston, the Fylde coast and, via the LNWR or Midland, to Scotland. Great Moor Street, on the other hand, at least as far as passenger traffic was concerned, had access to Manchester, North Wales via Manchester, the Leigh, Warrington and Wigan areas and Liverpool, as well as through coaches to Euston in LNWR days. That is, of course, a simplification, but it has implications for the services, the trains and their make-up, and the locomotives used.

While I have been careful to point out throughout this series that I have made no pretence of modelling Great Moor Street itself, I have used it as a source of inspiration for developing Platt Lane, not only in the planning of the layout, using features of the original such as the railway on the embankment and the coal drops next to the platform, but also the buildings and railway location in general. It seems therefore logical to follow this plagiarism of reality when looking at the trains and their operation. They will then be consistent with the model rather than a wish, impossible in reality, and will therefore hopefully add to the picture and impression I am trying to create. To understand the likely services and therefore the choice of locomotives and stock, it is necessary to delve a little bit into Great Moor Street's origins and how the line progressed and ultimately demised.

The railways to Bolton, and in particular what became the LNWR station in the town, provide a good example of the pattern of railway development in Britain.

The LNWR route owes its origin to the Bolton & Leigh Railway, which actually achieved its Act of Parliament in 1825, a year before the Liverpool & Manchester. This railway was promoted by a number of leading local industrialists that included prolific mining, cotton and engineering interests. Indeed, one of the promoters, John Hick, was to become a Director of the LNWR and have a class of locomotives named after him. He is also prominent on Platt Lane as one of the owners of the Bolton engineers, Hick, Hargreaves, whose frontage was conveniently moved to behind the station at Platt Lane.

The Bolton & Leigh opened its 7½ miles for freight-only use in 1828, and to passengers in 1831. It is interesting to note that at this juncture the promoters of the line hedged their bets, promoting the line as not only having a station in Bolton but also as being connected to the Bolton, Bury & Manchester Canal there, and at Leigh to the Leeds/Liverpool Canal. The Kenyon & Leigh Junction Railway Act of 1829 completed the connection to Liverpool, Warrington and, by a rather circuitous and long-winded route, to Manchester, Wigan and Preston.

That these early railways were promoted by local

industrialists is not surprising as the benefits were immense, for example reducing the price of coal in Bolton by 2 shillings a ton.

The railway at this time included two sections operated by stationary engines. A major disaster involving a runaway goods train that all but demolished the original Bolton station caused a rethink and, coupled with the interest of the local colliery-owning Hulton family in a new line from Manchester to Wigan by what had now become the LNWR, resulted in what became Great Moor Street.

The original, intended colliery spur off the Manchester-Wigan line, forming a junction at Roe Green to Little Hulton, was extended to Bolton. The new station, Great Moor Street, had four platforms 300 feet in length to serve trains not only to Liverpool via Leigh but now also to Manchester, into what would become Exchange station.

The canal interests rebutted by this railway promoted their own direct line between Manchester and Bolton. This ultimately joined other ventures linking Preston and Blackburn, promoting Bolton's other main station at Trinity Street and becoming part of the Lancashire & Yorkshire Railway.

Not surprisingly the promotion of, in particular, what became the LNWR routes by local businessmen led to the provision of extensive goods facilities ranging from colliery lines, coal sidings, numerous warehouses, goods yards, a brewery and several engineering works. Though there are now no collieries in the Lancashire coalfield, the area of south Lancashire from Liverpool to Salford once contained extensive colliery workings. Indeed, such workings were to result in the subsidence that led to the infamous Chequerbent incline, which when built at 1 in 45 was steep enough, but was increased to 1 in 18 in places as a result of subsidence!

You might ask what all this has to do with a model railway? Well, railways operated not for fun but for a purpose, and understanding that purpose and the consequent traffic in the area in which our model is based gives us the basis for the train services, and in turn the requirements for stock and locomotives to provide them. It ensures that our model is believable, gaining its credibility from reality rather than what we believe or assume reality to be. These aspects are, as I said earlier, just as important a part of the whole scene that we are creating as the buildings and scenic setting. Sometimes reality can lead to some very strange services and practices, but they are nevertheless credible on the layout because they are based on reality.

One example was the running of a through coach from Great Moor Street to London Euston via Manchester Exchange, the LNWR beating the time taken by the L&Y, which ran through services to the capital joining the London services at Stockport. Also Bacup, a small Lancashire & Yorkshire outpost in east Lancashire, referred to in previous volumes as another

possible inspiration for a model, originated a parcels train working to Stoke which shunted at Rochdale.

These types of working owed their origins to the way in which the railways developed, and lasted for many years. Indeed, it could be argued that, on the whole, the workings of

Left Push-pull-fitted Ivatt 2-6-2T No 41215 leaving Great Moor Street with a motor train in 1951. *Author's collection*

Below Another prototype inspiration - Fairburn 2-6-4T No 42051 stops at Gisburn on the L&Y's Blackburn-Hellifield line with a three-coach local, typical of the work these locos could be seen performing at the time of the Platt Lane layout. *Author's collection*

the railways remained little altered until the Beeching era. Perhaps the old adage 'If it ain't broke, don't fix it' applied. This does not, however, overlook the fact that lines and stations closed and services were rationalised to some degree before Beeching, but recognises that essentially the Victorian railway lasted until the 1960s.

Services on the prototype

As we have seen, Great Moor Street handled services to and from Manchester Exchange, North Wales and Liverpool via Kenyon Junction. Some incoming trains originated elsewhere, such as the 4.23 pm from Newton Le Willows, usually a motor-fitted train, which became the 4.29 Kenyon Junction to Bolton service.

The routes and services influenced the train formations and locomotives, and also the source of locomotives for these services. Great Moor Street eventually had its own shed, Plodder Lane, which opened in 1875 and closed in October 1954, some six months after the station itself. Originally Plodder Lane had been a sub-shed of Patricroft and was numbered 34P. After the LMS reorganisation it and Patricroft became sub-sheds of Springs Branch, becoming 10D, 10B and 10A respectively. Incidentally, Plodder Lane was, I believe, unique in having half its allocation replaced at once by new locomotives, Ivatt 2-6-2 tank locomotives for LNWR coal tanks, in 1949.

Though Plodder Lane provided some motive power for ex-Great Moor Street services, it did not by any means provide it all. The first two morning days from Manchester Exchange were powered by Patricroft Stanier 2-6-4Ts. The stock from the first went back to Exchange on the 7.25 from Great Moor Street powered by a Plodder Lane '4F' 0-6-0 or LNWR 0-8-0 on weekdays and an Ivatt 2-6-2T on Saturday; obviously during the week the goods engine had 'business' to da around Manchester. Local memories tell of the plum 'turn' for Plodder Lane men being the crewing of a Patricroft 'Precursor' on North Wales excursion services. There was much heavy coal traffic on the lines surrounding Great Moor Street and this was usually the responsibility of either Patricroft or Springs branch locos.

At the Grouping in 1923 Plodder Lane operated over 30 locos on local freight and passenger duties, but the formation of the LMS in that year the close proximity of Horwich Works and the large Bolton L&Y shed led to the local ascendency of that company's locomotive operation base in the area. However, Great Moor Street was isolated from the L&Y system locally except by colliery lines, which were hardly

suitable for regular usage by main-line locomotives, and the nearest 'interchange' between the two systems was at Eccles or Wigan, so Plodder Lane shed maintained its role until the end of Great Moor Street.

Services on the model

Again, this is all very interesting, but what has it got to do with our model railway, you may think. Well, even though we haven't modelled Great Moor Street, we have modelled an LNWR terminus in south Lancashire, serving an industrial town. It is therefore reasonable to assume that such a station would run services to Manchester and Liverpool and would deserve some locomotive facilities a la Plodder Lane. If we are to continue to look to reality to steer us in the right direction for our model, we could do worse than study the Great Moor Street services, formations and locomotives.

Once again this is a practice that I would suggest can be used wherever and whenever your model is set. The information is reasonably straightforward to obtain if we take the trouble to look, from books, photographs, local histories, local libraries, and books on the practices and developments of the railway companies, all of which can inform our choices. In fact it is exactly this same process we used to build the layout.

The thing about research is that it is something we can do from the comfort of our armchair. There is nothing more therapeutic than whiling away time sketching out possible ideas for a layout, railway lines that might have been, possible extensions or variations. This armchair modelling, much derided, can be very entertaining, and if you are prepared to look out for appropriate books and magazines, which are now available in abundance, you don't have to do much work - sounds like my kind of modelling. . . Research is an aspect that I think is much underrated; is very interesting and can be a rewarding pastime on its own without the need to produce the sort of information needed for a detailed history. Indeed, I think the reality and the image or impression behind the stark statistics and facts are far more fascinating and certainly gives a better 'feel' for things.

Though Great Moor Street closed in 1954, adjacent goods facilities and the coal drops were still in use until 1963 and the station was used for excursion traffic, and particularly 'Wakes Weeks' services to North Wales, until 1959. This adds a slight problem in that while it is fairly easy to deduce appropriate stock and locomotives for this line before 1954, as the layout is set later, circa 1959/60, given the demise of

The humble 'trip' working is often ignored by modellers in favour of the pick-up goods. The trip working is essentially movement of freight from major yards to smaller local yards for loading and unloading and the transfer of vehicles to larger yards for making up freight trains for the onward-bound journey. Such duties were often the preserve of antiquated locomotives and could comprise anything from a couple of wagons upwards, and are much more convenient for a layout such as Platt Lane than the archetypal pick-up goods, collecting and dropping off vehicles en route from A to B at a leisurely pace.

It can readily be assumed that as the major Platt Lane goods facilities are 'off stage', conveniently small trains would bring in and out vehicles for Bollings Yard and the coal drops; the few wagons for the latter would come into the area on longer coal trains, and would be cut out and dispatched as a trip working to the drops, as a separate exercise and probably from a different yard from those for Bollings yard.

It was common for older locomotives to finish their days on this type of work, but although the trip workings were regularly diagrammed and could involve some shunting, in fact the locos provided were often what was left, and in times of engine shortages some very surprising locomotives could turn up. Shown here, for example, is an ex-L&YR Aspinall saddle tank collecting its train for a trip working at Bolton in July 1960. *D. Hampson*

in the hands of Sutton Oak (St Helens) locomotives. If we make that assumption it helps with the choice of locomotives, as we can quite easily find out what these sheds had on their books and how things changed, as change they did quite rapidly in the last few years of steam.

Therefore going back to the general traffic requirements, the conclusions to which I came for Platt Lane were that for the period of the layout passenger services would be provided to Manchester (Exchange) and to Liverpool, the two major North West conurbations. Remember that the LNWR, the builders of our line, were great operators of connecting services and often provided short services that connected with others going to the ultimate destination. Thus at Great Moor Street, rather than a direct service from Bolton to Liverpool it may have been Bolton to Kenyon Junction and a change there to a Manchester-Liverpool service. Regular Great Moor Street to Kenyon Junction services ran throughout the line's life and were, certainly in the late LMS and BR days, operated primarily but by no means exclusively by 'motor' (push-pull) trains. It would be reasonable to assume therefore that some of the services operated on the layout would be typical LNWR connecting services and, as I commented earlier, there is every chance that these would have continued until the Beeching era. This gives me an excuse, or rather a reason, to run a motor train service as my connecting service to Liverpool and the direct service to Manchester. This outlined scenario is just one possibility deduced from reality; there are of course others based on interesting 'might have beens'.

Movement of freight was the prime motivation for the original Bolton & Leigh line to Great Moor Street. If you look at the sponsors of the line, and indeed the facilities provided, you get a good indication of the freight traffic - coal, engineering, general merchandise and a brewery, which even up to the mid-'60s, when it ceased brewing, had a rather unusual traffic - of which more later.

Platt Lane has the equivalent (though much reduced) of 'Mr Hulton's coal sidings', which were adjacent to Great Moor Street. Several other sid-

pre-Grouping coach types during this period, the closure of facilities and the re-allocation of locomotives, more assumptions have to be made by reference to known local practices on similar lines in the area, in particular shed allocations and photographs of that period.

It is quite possible that even had Great Moor Street remained open until 1959/60 for regular services, Plodder Lane would still have been closed in 1954. If that was the case, then locomotives would have been diagrammed from Patricroft and Springs Branch primarily, but also from other sheds; for example, some Kenyon Junction to Great Moor Street services were

ings in the area served engineering works, and it can be assumed that somewhere, perhaps 'off stage', is a siding serving our engineering works of J. M. Hargreaves. The coal sidings would clearly bring in coal for bagging, distribution and sale by local merchants. Bollings Yard would provide for general merchandise at a small local level away from the major facilities, equivalent to Crook Street Yard and Warehouses close to Great Moor Street, again

assumed to be 'off stage'. There would of course also be what might be loosely termed 'van traffic'. There was, in the period of our layout, quite a considerable parcels traffic in the area of our model.

That then is the background to the provision of locomotives and rolling-stock for Platt Lane. In a moment we will look at how these requirements can be met by commercially available kits, but first a few words on modelling techniques.

Platt Lane comes to life: as the model nears completion, here's a busy shunting scene featuring Fairburn 2-6-4T No 42185, L&Y '27' Class 0-6-0 No 52447 and a collection of freight stock.

2.
MODELLING TECHNIQUES

You don't need a well-equipped workshop to assemble loco and rolling-stock kits - literally the kitchen table will suffice. A word of caution, though: if domestic harmony is to be maintained, it is a good idea to have a piece of blockboard or similar as your work surface to prevent damage to the table or kitchen worktop. This could, if necessary, be clamped down, remembering of course to protect the top from the clamp jaws with a piece of felt or similar. This could also be developed into a complete portable workshop, housing tools, bits and pieces and its own power supply; there have been a few detailed articles in the model press over recent years on constructing this type of facility.

However, first let's look at a basic list of 'bare essential' tools, from which no doubt your tool kit will grow gradually as your interest develops.

Tools and equipment

Not all the tools listed below are essential, but they will all help to facilitate good modelling. Remember, however, one golden rule: cheap tools are a false economy. Always buy the best you can afford, because not only will good tools last longer, they will also give you better results and certainly cause less frustration in their use. Cheap 50p pliers that don't close accurately and evenly will not only give poor results but will be frustrating to use, and possibly even dangerous.

Because good tools are not cheap they should be regarded as an asset and investment, and looked after properly. Keep them clean and keep them sharp. It is less likely that accidents will occur using sharp cutting tools than when trying to force blunt ones. Replacement knife and saw blades are cheap enough. Replacement fingers? Well. . .

My suggested list of tools is as follows:

Craft knife A sharp knife and a good supply of blades are essential for plastic kits. Blunt knife blades can be dangerous as there is a temptation to apply a bit more pressure to complete the cut, which can quite easily result in the blade braking and the sharp fragment fly-

The basic tool kit for assembling a plastic wagon kit. A sharp knife and a good supply of blades is essential, as is a selection of files and fine abrasive material such as OO wet and dry paper for cleaning up components prior to assembly and to ensure a good fit; time and care spent here is well rewarded later in the finished model. All joints between plastic components are made with a liquid solvent. It is often necessary, however, to fix components made from other materials such as white metal or brass, and here 'superglue' is usually adequate, though there may be occasions when epoxy resin adhesive is more appropriate.

Some means of making holes is also useful, for handrails, door handles, etc, which are often not moulded in the kit components, or if they are they may need to be opened out; a small modeller's minidrill will do the trick. This tool has the advantage of flexibility, its use being extended to power small cutters, grindstones and polishing wheels, and it comes into its own when making metal kits or laying track.

I always find it useful to have a steel rule handy, both to check measurements if I am to modify anything, and to check for straightness or to provide a guide for cutting straight lines. A small engineer's square is similarly useful and, with a fine brush to apply liquid solvent to the plastic components, completes the basic tool kit.

ing away from the work with surprising ferocity, usually in the direction of the user, with painful consequences!

Just occasionally a heavier knife is called for and a Stanley DIY knife, again with a good supply of sharp blades is handy. This type of knife is a useful addition to the modeller's tool kit anyway.

Swiss or needle files These are usually available in sets of five or six, but can be bought individually. I find flat, round and half round most useful. If used on white metal castings or for removing excess solder they quickly become clogged, but cleaning them with a wire brush will sort this out. Because good-quality needle files are quite expensive I usually keep old worn ones or even buy cheap ones for use on white metal or for the cleaning of excess solder, etc.

Pliers Small, long-nose pliers are essential for bending handrails, etc, and a general-purpose or 'engineer's' pair is also useful.

Drills A supply of small twist drill bits will be essential. Usually handrail knobs and grab rails need to be drilled with a No 68 bit, and No 55 is for 10 BA screws and bolts. Other sizes can be bought as you need them if you don't buy a drill set. If you do buy a set, buy the set covering sizes in the 68 to 50 range, which will suffice for most purposes. These small drills are comparatively expensive and obviously fragile, so keep them clean and sharp and don't force them, particularly if drilling cast metal, as they can easy become stuck and 'lost' in the casting; then not only do you have a broken drill, but also the nigh-on-impossible task of drilling the hole accurately.

Pin chuck This is a small chuck, sometimes with alternative-sized collets, which will hold the very small drills we need to use. It enables a hole to be made by hand by twisting and rotating the bit between the fingers and thumb. A pin chuck can be used in a hand drill or even a power drill, but will require great care to ensure that the drill is kept square and no pressure is exerted. A pin chuck comes into its own when drilling in plastic.

Mini drill There are a number of these on the market and they are so versatile a tool that I would consider them as essential. If you have a mini drill, a pin chuck is not essential. Operating from your controller on 12V DC or from their own transformer, they can be used for drilling, sawing, cutting, grinding and polishing, and some systems even have their own vertical drill stands, milling attachments and the like.

Screwdrivers A set of jeweller's screwdrivers, sold in plastic wallets containing four or five different types will suffice. One or two 'Phillips' type would be a useful addition, particularly for the fixing of the mounting bracket screws in Japanese motors.

Soldering iron For soldering white metal, a low-wattage or a temperature-controlled iron is essential, while for etched kits and certainly sheet metal an iron of substantial wattage is needed. There is an extensive range on the market. I have a 25-watt iron that I use for white metal and finer etched and sheet parts, and a now rather old 80-watt iron that I have found to be the master of anything I've needed to solder in 7 mm scale. There are a number of pocket gas torches on the market, and while fine for electrical work or spot soldering, I find them inappropriate for most of the soldering encountered in the building of locomotives.

Burnishing tool This is essential to clean and polish white metal and brass/nickel parts prior to painting. The pencil type with refills are most suitable, but the most economical are the bound sticks 3 or 4 inches long, available from jewellers' suppliers.

Vice I hesitate to suggest that a vice is essential, but it is one of those tools that once you have one you can't understand how you managed without it! It is handy for holding white metal while it is filed and cut, holding sheet or etched metal parts while being bent, and of course for holding parts while being soldered. A vice with jaws opening up to 3 or 4 inches will suffice even for O gauge. It is essential to ensure that the jaws close accurately together.

Try square A small engineers's square is very useful for checking the squareness of components and assemblies such as cabs or tank sides.

Razor saw For fine cuts in thin metal and plastic, the type with interchangeable or replacement blades such as the X Acto is best.

Taps Taper taps of 8 and 10 BA for 4 mm, and 6 and 8 BA in 7 mm scale, enable threads to be tapped into parts to enable fixing by bolts. Often a nut can be soldered over a pre-drilled clearance hole to avoid using a tap.

G clamps Miniature G clamps are available in sets of three and may be useful to hold certain parts together.

Hair clips These and similar items are useful for holding parts when soldering and are sometimes referred to as heat sinks.

Junior hacksaw This can be useful for cutting heavier metals such as frame brass, etc.

Callipers/dividers These are useful in scratchbuilding and in extensive kit modification to transfer dimensions from a drawing.

Wet and dry papers Medium to fine grades can be used for finishing parts before assembly and in final preparation before painting.

There will be other tools and pieces of equipment that you will find useful as your expertise develops and you find your own methods. For example, I keep broken and blunted craft knife blades for scraping solder and paring down white metal. Old toothbrushes are useful for cleaning up models prior to painting, and as mentioned above I find hairclips useful for holding small parts together while soldering. Blue-Tack is similarly useful.

Soldering

If you are building a model railway then sooner or later the need to solder will arise. There have been several learned treatises in the model press on the technicalities of soft soldering, and the next few paragraphs are intended as a brief practical guide to the essentials. If you have any doubts, practice on some scrap metal - cut up a tin can or whatever. But do have a go - it is not nearly as difficult as it seems.

As with most aspects of model building there are a few basic principles. The first runs common to many other aspects of modelling, and this is cleanliness. The metal to be joined must be clean and grease-free where the solder is to run, so clean the parts in this area with wet and dry or the burnishing tool.

The second is the right solder for the job. Basically the choice is between multicore solder for sheet and etched metal kits and low-melt solder for white metal kits. However, there are now a number of solders on the market, such as the Carrs range, which offer a variety of melting point temperatures. These possess certain advantages where a number of parts are built up to form detail, where it is useful not to have need of so much heat when fixing the last part that the other parts in the assembly become unsoldered.

The third essential is to have sufficient heat for the job in hand. It is no good in O gauge trying to solder $\frac{1}{16}$ inch brass to brass frame spacers with a 25-watt iron. Conversely, apply too much heat to white metal and instead of a set of nicely detailed cast parts you'll have a pool of molten alloy!

Flux is needed to wipe the intended joint where the solder will flow, and a mild flux is formulated specifically for modelling. It is a very mild acid but, even though a weak solution, is still potentially dangerous, being both corrosive and poisonous. Whatever you do, do not be tempted to use Bakers Fluid, Yorkshire Flux Paste or other such fluxes commonly available at DIY stores, as these are very corrosive and

intended for industrial and plumbing uses. You can get a very good joint using these, but don't be surprised if the metal is eaten away shortly afterwards! In soldering sheet or etched metal, ordinary multicore solder is sufficient.

We'll have a look now at these principles in a bit more detail. Before soldering kit components, practise a simple 90-degree joint. Cut a couple of pieces of scrap material and check that the two parts are a good and accurate fit, square and true. A simple wooden jig is helpful to hold them at 90 degrees while the hot iron is applied, and it is worth spending a few minutes in preparation. It saves a lot of burnt fingers!

Clean the edges to be soldered and wipe them with flux with a small brush. Take each piece separately and hold the iron on the edge where the flux has been applied, then bring the solder to the iron where it touches the metal and, moving the iron along the edge, coat the edge with a thin, even film of solder. Smooth out any blobs with the iron but be careful not to add more solder than necessary - a thin even coating is all that is required. This process is known as tinning.

Now position the parts against the wooden jig as they are to be assembled, hold the iron on the joint and slide it steadily along its length. The solder from the previously tinned edges should flow together and, when the iron is removed and the metal allowed to cool for a few seconds, the joint should be made. It's as simple as that. It is quite possible to add more solder and flux to make the joint should this be necessary, but if you tinned the parts properly you shouldn't need to.

It is not always possible to tin the components before assembly, so in this case the parts are held together, the joint wiped with flux, the iron applied, and solder introduced to the iron, which is drawn along the joint.

When it comes to soldering small parts - for example tank front steps into slots in the tank front - it will be sufficient to add the solder to the heated joint surfaces, rather than tin them. In many instances it will be sufficient to merely touch the joint for a few seconds, providing that it is well fluxed and only a very small amount of solder will be required.

The most common failure of soldered joints is what is known as a 'dry joint'. This is invariably because the joint has not been heated enough for the solder to flow correctly, or it has been moved before it has cooled sufficiently for the solder to harden. It is easy to tell if the solder is hot enough and therefore flowing correctly, because it will become a bright shiny silver; as it cools it becomes more grey in colour.

Solder assembly of white metal kits is altogether different. Because the melting point of the cast metal is low, great care needs to be taken to avoid melting the components along with the solder. The melting point of ordinary solder is higher than that of the casting, therefore special low-melting-point solder is called for, along with a low-wattage iron. For safety's sake I confine soldering white metal kits to the main structural components, using 'superglue' for finer parts and details.

The basic soldering procedure outlined above is followed, although I find that rather than tinning the parts it is easier to introduce the low-melt solder to the fluxed joint along with the iron. The trick is to allow the iron to be there just long enough for the solder to flow; the soldering iron needs to be moved away very rapidly to avoid melting adjacent parts if you are working in a confined area, such as inside a tank or cab.

I find it easier and safer to use my 25-watt iron quickly than a smaller iron for longer, on the basis that the hotter iron, moved quickly, gives less heat build-up than the smaller iron used for longer periods on the same spot. I don't know whether there is any scientific support for this theory, but it is just my preference. I guess that it stems from learning the method before the many varieties of low-melt solders and such items as variable-temperature irons were readily available to modellers!

There will be occasions when it is necessary to solder white metal parts to sheet metal. Here the procedure is to tin the sheet metal with low-melt solder, apply flux to this area, hold the cast component in place and, by holding the iron on the sheet metal adjacent to, but not near enough to melt, the casting, 'sweat' the casting on (ie hold it into the molten tin-

Beading is being 'sweated' on to this cab roof as described in the text. Note the tinning on the underside of the section about to be fixed.

ning). Then remove the iron and allow the joint to cool. The most common use for this type of joint is fixing white metal chimneys and domes on to brass boilers.

Glues

Inevitably there are occasions when it is not possible to solder metal kit components and some form of glue has to be used. The glues we might use are either epoxy resins or 'superglue'. These glues are essential if fixing in place parts made from other materials, for example plastic.

The epoxy resins come in two types: quick-drying (5 minutes) and the 24-hour-cure types. There is no doubt in my experience that the 24-hour type gives a stronger bond, and such glues are useful when strength rather than appearance is the main requirement. However, it is seldom convenient to wait a long time for the glue to cure.

Epoxy adhesives are mixed from two different chemicals to produce the 'glue', which inevitably is a thick substance precluding fine, accurate assembly. However, where appearance is not a consideration, such as fixing cast bogie mounting points to the underside of coach bogies, they are superior to the 'superglues'. For the glue to be most effective the parts to be assembled should be clean and free from grease or dirt and left undisturbed until the glue has set.

'Superglues' are almost instant, and require only the tiniest spot to effect a strong joint. They are thus ideal where quality of fit is required, or for fixing fine detail. They will also stick most materials to each other (and you, so be careful!). They do, however, require scrupulous cleanliness if the glue is to be effective. Clean the parts and ensure that you don't touch the area that will be affected by the glue as even the natural grease from your skin will affect the quality of the joint.

This type of glue is now available in liquid and gels and in various types of dispenser. I prefer the liquid applied by a pin - only a touch is required, from a straightforward, no-gimmick pack.

A word of warning, however: heat will destroy the glued joint, and in the process of degenerating under heat the glue lets off very nasty and poisonous fumes which I believe are similar to the gases used in the trenches in the First World War! Therefore avoid soldering anything near a superglued joint, which means planning your sequence of construction so that you solder first and glue last.

In contrast, heat actually speeds up the curing time of epoxy glues, but I wouldn't risk putting parts in a warm oven unless you are sure that they won't be damaged. Perhaps more importantly, as Rumpole might say, have the permission of 'she who must be obeyed'.

To recap, the key elements for the successful use of 'superglue' are:

Cleanliness - ensure that the surfaces to be joined are spotlessly clean and above all free from grease. Run the burnishing tool over the surfaces to be bonded and don't touch them or put them on an oily work bench.

Quality of fit - the glue won't fill gaps in joints between components, therefore you need to ensure that parts are well prepared to fit together and are held steady and in a good tight fit for a few seconds until the glue sets.

Quantity - the more glue you use the longer it takes to cure, the weaker the joint and less is the certainty of success. Put a pinhead's worth on a non-porous piece of scrap, dip the point of a pin into it and apply the glue to the surfaces to be bonded.

Kit preparation

Cutting and fixing plastic

If your modelling experience to date has not gone much beyond assembling plastic aircraft or tank kits, don't worry - if you have assembled them accurately you will be able to manage at least the plastic wagon kits we will building in the next chapter.

So far as the removal of parts from sprues is concerned, this is perhaps the most crucial operation as, if you don't remove them carefully, you will damage the parts and thus risk detracting from the appearance of the finished model. Forget any ideas of breaking off or twisting out parts from the sprues - cut them carefully.

For this you will need a sharp craft knife. Place the sprue on something solid to make the cut. If you can't get them on a flat cutting board, support fine parts of complex shapes that fall below or above the sprues, for example brake parts, on something improvised, such as a can or additional block of wood, to prevent them from breaking. Be prepared for several light cuts rather than one hefty blow! I usually keep a Stanley knife handy for cutting out larger, thicker parts. Again, ensure that the blade is sharp.

Clean the remnants of the sprues on the components by scraping the edges with a knife and finishing with fine wet and dry paper. Try to avoid marking the external surfaces.

If you are using sheet plastic you will need to cut it to fabricate the required components, such as a wagon floor or roof, or to make parts to provide variations on the vehicle supplied in the kit.

The first thing is to ensure that your cutting is square, and to do this you need a true 90-degree set of lines from which to mark out your parts. Don't assume that the edges of a sheet of plastic are square! Draw a straight line the length of, and close to, one edge, then cut it by scoring the line and breaking off the edge - you only need a millimetre or so. If the ruler shows the edge to be straight, mark it with a marking pen and use an engineer's square to mark off a line at 90 degrees close to another edge. Check this for accuracy and mark the accurate line. You now have a checked 90-degree angle from which to work to ensure that your components are square.

Cutting sheet plastic is easy. Use a sharp knife and a steel rule to guide the blade. For curves you can purchase quite cheaply compass cutters from Kirtley Models.

In plastic up to about 20 thou thick, the cut is likely to go through the plastic; where it doesn't it can be broken off.

For thicker plastic, score the line and snap the pieces off. Obviously the thicker the plastic, the deeper the scoring needed. Also you will find that when cutting thick plastic, burrs will be left that will need to be cleaned off with a few strokes of wet and dry; wrap the paper around a block of wood if it's a long strangle cut.

When it comes to joining, forget the old tubes of polystyrene cement - there is no place for that in our modelling. Instead we will need to use one of the liquid solvents such

The basics of a typical plastic wagon kit, in this case a Parkside Dundas LMS design box van.

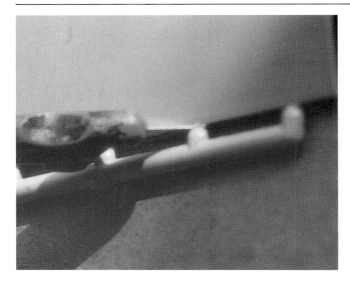

Goods wagons on a model railway are viewed from a rather unnaturally high level. Accordingly, great care is necessary to ensure, for example, that van roofs are a good fit and clean and unblemished; extra care is needed in cleaning edges and removing moulding pips on van roofs and the upper edges of open wagon sides. The first picture shows careful cutting of the roof from the sprue - whatever you do, don't break it off. The second shows the roof removed and the typical remains left to be cleaned off.

as Mek Pac or Liquid Poly. These will fix the plastic in most kits, but some plastics, particularly those used for some of the structural parts such as Plas Struc, will need a special adhesive. However, I believe that these products are now being made from polystyrene like the kits. The best way to ensure that you have the right solvent is to enquire when you purchase your plastic.

These liquid solvents are applied sparingly with a fine brush into the joint to be made. This means that you need to ensure that the parts fit cleanly and accurately before you apply the solvent. Keep the components together for a couple of minutes until the solvent has dried - to aid accurate assembly use jigs and supports as suggested for soldering.

Because the solvent is liquid and flows freely, it will flow through gaps, so when you are holding parts together, ensure that it doesn't flood through to the outside around your fingers and leave your fingerprints indelibly moulded on the outside of your model!

Assembling and using plastic is as simple as that; as always a little care, patience and thought is all that is required. Be careful with the solvents, however; they evaporate very quickly, so keep the lid on tightly. I suspect that breathing their fumes in a confined space won't do you any good, either. Oh, and if they will melt plastic they won't do clothes, furniture or carpets any good, so as with all modelling materials, treat them carefully and with respect.

Preparing metal parts

Most etched components need to be removed from frets, like removing the plastic components from sprues. Again, care is needed if the parts are not to be damaged.

For thicker components with large tabs holding them to the frets, fine tinsnips are useful; cut away from the edge of the part and clean up with a file afterwards. For smaller, thin parts, often a sharp knife will do the trick; cut against a cutting board and you can use the knife as a chisel. Don't try to cut the part out exactly as you will be more likely to damage it; leave a slight distance from the edge where you cut, and again clean the piece with needle files to the final outline. It sounds complicated but it isn't really - it is more a question of patience in the rush of enthusiasm to get started.

I tend to remove the parts from the fret only as I need them, but sometimes, for example in assembling the brakes on the Aspinall 0-6-0 to be encountered later, I will cut the parts out and fabricate these sub-assemblies in one go, then put them away in a plastic 35mm film tub or similar container.

White metal needs in essence to be treated in a similar way to plastic components because we are cleaning away any moulding flash and excess metal. Again it is a matter of carefully scraping away flash with a knife and finishing with very fine wet and dry.

I tend to avoid filing white metal as it clogs files, but as it is sometimes unavoidable, for example when filing inaccessible parts without damaging nearby detail such as rivets, I keep a few old, cheap needle files for this purpose.

The most important tool is the fibreglass burnishing tool; lightly rubbing it over the model will smooth the surface and remove any remnants of mould release powders, but applied a bit more vigorously it can polish out many surface imperfections.

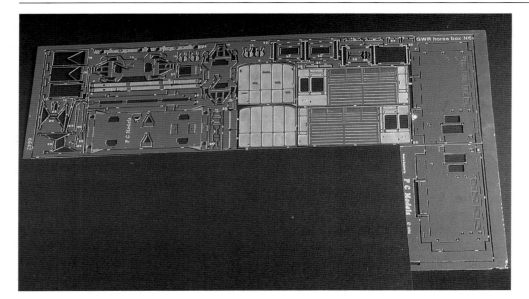

Components of the PC Models etched brass GWR horsebox kit - hardly 'shake the box and it's assembled'! I am not convinced that etched brass is the most appropriate medium for wagon kits, but it is an economic fact of life that it is often the only commercially viable means of producing vehicles that are only likely to sell in comparatively small quantities. Carefully made, good etched-kit-based wagons are a joy for the wealth of detail they can offer, as in the completed Fruit D shown below. Castings are supplied for some of the details but the main components for the vehicle are on this fret.

One final point on etched kits: the frets surrounding the parts provide a good supply of scrap material, which is worth cutting into convenient lengths and putting away. This material can often provide the basis for additional details; thin strips can become the basis of lamp brackets, for example.

Body matters

Sub-assemblies

Squareness and accuracy is essential for the finished appearance of the model. One way of helping this is almost a side benefit of a way of construction that lends itself to the design of several of the kits we will be looking at for Platt Lane. Essentially, this is the process of building up the model from several sub-assemblies. This usually arises from building a model with a complicated livery, where it becomes easier to paint and line the model in bits rather than as a whole, as it were. If you are building up the model from sub-assemblies, they have to be square and true so that they will fit

well together and thus produce a square and true finished model.

Boiler fittings

Chimneys, domes, etc, *must* sit down flush, neatly and accurately on the smokebox and boiler, and there are many ways that we can help this process.

One is to run the component with its underside down along a suitable diameter dowel or oddment of tube that has a piece of wet and dry wrapped around it. The second is to roll the edges down carefully with a piece of steel rod or similar. Whatever you do, ensure that the components are applied vertically and centred - nothing jars more on the eye than a leaning chimney!

Beading, cab window frames, boiler bands, steps and sub-assemblies

Applying boiler bands, beading and cab windows in etched kits can cause a few moments' terror to the uninitiated. It is, however, a relatively simple operation providing that you tin the beading first, proceed in a logical, steady way, and follow the basic soldering principles outlined above.

Sometimes on earlier period locos, cab window frames were left polished brass and, if that is the finish you want and a separate etching is provided, it is best applied to the model after painting.

Boiler bands are a little different, but the basic principle is the same as with beading: tin the band, pre-curve it and apply the flux and hot iron along its length. On the real thing the ends are bent at 90 degrees and a bolt runs through to tighten them on the cladding. This can be represented by cutting the bands slightly over length and bending the ends to 90 degrees. Whatever you do with the bands, ensure that they are vertical and evenly spaced.

Steps are always vulnerable on models and I think it is always worthwhile providing hidden support where possible. In fact, on the real thing many steps had supporting brackets behind them, so why not copy reality?

Cab roofs

On tank locomotives it is not unusual to find an enclosed cab that consequently makes internal detailing and painting difficult. The answer is a simple one - make the roof removable. The accompanying photograph shows a simple arrangement that is ideal for tank locomotives with more modern, rounded cab roofs. This is simply a piece of bent rod and spring used to make a locating pin that is held in place in a frame of scrap brass. The housing is a washer soldered on the cab front or rear plate. The other locating pin is simply a piece of brass rod. The most complex part of the procedure is lining up the pins with the housings. This is done by holding the roof in its correct position and turning the loco body upside down; a marker pen is then used to mark both the inside cab front and rear and the roof. It is not necessary to mark a line continuously along the roof, merely to mark the point where roof and cab front/rear meet as near to the centre as possible. This gives the point at which to fix the locating pins or bolts and their housings.

One alternative idea more suited to older types is a simple clip made from diagonal pieces of wire with the ends bent round. They should be sufficiently long to pro-

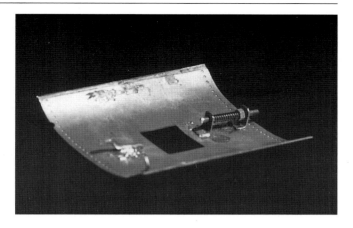

Cab roofs should ideally be removable to allow detailing of the interior. The simple spring catch made from scrap material and the peg at the other end are designed to locate in either a pre-drilled holes in the cab front and back or, better still as they are completely hidden, washers soldered on the inside.

duce a tight fit between roof and sides, and are marked out (corners only necessary) as in the previous method.

The chassis

Wheels and crank pins

There is cause for little comment here, save to ensure that with metal wheels the insulated ends are all on

Right One problem encountered with all locos with outside valve gear is the limited room behind the slide bars and the difficulty in getting the crank pins on the leading driver to clear the slide bars. One easy way to counter this is to put spacing washers behind the leading driver to eliminate side-play.

Below right The three main contenders for driving wheels in O gauge. On the left is a traditional cast iron wheel with a steel shouldered crank pin fitted from the outside through the rod. Insulation is achieved by either cutting through the spokes and filling the gap with Araldite or, as here, turning off the tyre from the wheel, replacing it and holding it in place with Araldite. These processes are also carried out by the manufacturer. The wheels on the right are Slaters, and fit on to square-ended axles to assist with 'quartering'; they consist of a brass centre located in the moulded boss and spokes, and a steel rim. Crank pins are fitted from the rear, and rods are held in place by nuts. The centre wheels are by Alan Gibson; they have cast centres and steel rims, and are insulated at the axle end. The axles are telescopic and the pin illustrated locks the axles in position, correctly quartered. As with the Slaters wheels, these are for specific locomotives rather than general wheels based on size.

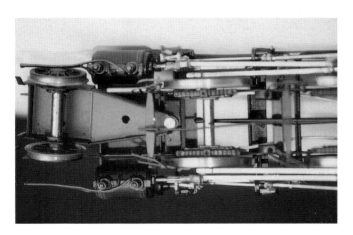

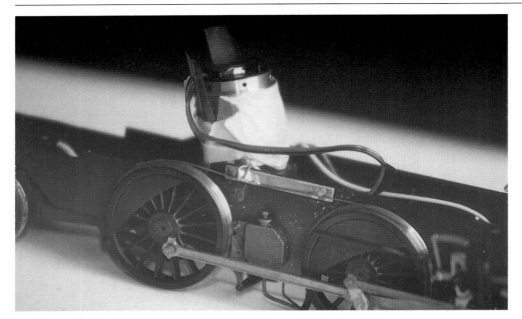

Left Pick-ups come in all shapes, sizes and methods. Here is an example of the way I arrange wiper contacts, suspended from a copper-clad sleeper strip and bearing down on the wheel treads. Note the tape around the motor and contacts to prevent them from accidentally touching the firebox sides.

Below left An alternative method is the plunger pick-up. The sprung plunger contacts are seen here within the chassis of the L&Y 0-6-0 saddle tank described later in the book.

thickness of the rod plus the rim, place a 14 BA washer between wheel and rod and solder - carefully - the rim of the bush to the crank pin. Obviously, if you're going to do this you can't easily remove the rod, so ensure that everything else is OK first.

The second problem of fixing the return crank to the crank pin is down to deft use of the soldering iron, but most important is the need to ensure the correct angle of the return crank.

the same side. As other types are by their nature insulated on non-metal spokes it does not matter.

Cast iron wheels generally have crank pins applied from the outside whereas, for example, the Slaters wheels shown in the accompanying photograph have the crank pins inserted from the rear.

The main problems with crank pins are ensuring on locos with outside valve gear that the leading pin does not foul the crosshead and/or connecting rod, and in the fixing of the return crank. There are two basic types: those used for cast iron wheels usually incorporate one special pin that has a very thin head to help with the clearance problem. With the other type, the normal arrangement with a nut is usually too thick to give adequate clearance. One method on Slaters wheels is to turn the 'top hat' bush used on the crank pin upside down so that the pin is outermost. File the length of the bush so that it is the same as the

Pick-ups

Perhaps the most common reason for problems with the running of locomotives relates to current collection. There are two basic methods: one is the wiper system, using some form of wire or strip that bears on the wheels, either on the tread or behind the rim. This is the traditional method and will suit most applications.

However, this system is now much criticised by those who favour more modern applications such as plunger pick-ups. Many kits and commercial milled chassis, such as the Wigan Wagon Works O gauge range, make provision for these and include them. I use both systems and, providing that they are installed with some care, they are unobtrusive and equally effective.

When installing plungers, ensure that the spring and tail of the brass plunger are lightly oiled, but *don't*

This chassis kit provides for the brakes to be hung from pivots that are insulated from the chassis, helping to ensure that even if the brakes touch the wheel rims they won't short on the chassis. An added precaution against shorting out is carefully to smear a film of Evo-Stik or Araldite over the edge of the brake shoe where it will might come in contact with the wheel.

use grease, which attracts dirt that will eventually prevent the easy movement of the plunger necessary for effective working. Similarly, ensure that only a very fine, flexible wire is used to connect the plunger to the motor and that this is soldered to the end of the tail, not to its side, otherwise again free movement may be impaired.

Brake and sanding gear

There is nothing complicated here either, just a question of patience. Not long ago few models had brake and sanding gear, but now they look rather bare and, indeed, few models in 4 or 7 mm scales are seen without them.

The main general problems as I see it are locating the brake gear where no provision is made in the chassis, and ensuring that it does not short on the wheels, yet doesn't leave a yawning gap between wheel and brake-shoe. The danger of shorting is simply overcome by smearing Araldite *neatly* along the edge and back of the shoe, thus providing some insulation. We will look at brake gear in more detail when we build some of the locomotives later.

Sanding gear is sometimes provided for in kits, generally where there are large sand boxes on the frames from which pipes emerge, and castings are supplied for this. Otherwise you are left on your own, possibly with a bit of wire. No problem - remember that sand pipes are generally quite thick, and to be effective must go down to somewhere near rail level. Simply bend the wire with a U at the top, which simultaneously gives the spacing from frame to wheel tread and provides a point at which to solder the pipe to the frames.

A final point: make sure that the pipes line up with any sand box fillers or lids on the footplate or splashers, and look out for those that thread their way through the brake rigging.

Valve gear

There is little call for comment here as the valve gear assembly will be covered later when discussing the locomotives being built for the layout. The main thing to remember is the sequence of fitting the rods, which are generally assembled on small 12, 14 and 16 BA nuts and bolts as pins. Generally pins are essential with etched valve gear and must be soldered to one rod and cut. The latter operation is easiest with a cutting disc in a mini drill.

Obviously when soldering the pins in place it is essential to avoid the rods being soldered together, so be *very* sparing with the flux. A tiny smear of petroleum jelly on the inside of the surfaces helps prevent accidental soldering; perhaps easiest of all is a strip of *thin* paper, effectively a washer, which can be removed when the joint is complete. Joints must be free enough to allow easy movement, but *must not be sloppy*.

Be careful when cutting down bolts and pins or filing or grinding down nut and bolt heads, as much of the milled valve gear is actually plated to give it its finish, and if you want to preserve this finish you will need to avoid scratching the plating away.

On crossheads and slide bars, again accuracy and free movement without any 'slop' is essential. Usually the problem is getting the crosshead to move smoothly, and this is generally down to the guides cast into the crosshead, which, even on the better 'lost wax' examples, need a bit of attention with the files to clean out the surfaces that bear and guide the part on the slide bar.

It is also helpful to polish the piston rod to ensure smooth operation and improve its appear-

The coupling rods of the Ivatt Class '2' kit are jointed on the centre axle to enable the chassis to be compensated or sprung, and provision is made in the design to fit Slater's hornblocks.

ance, as on the real thing it would be steel polished from use. Don't forget that you will probably also have to trim the piston rod to length so that when the crank pin is at its nearest to the cylinder the rod doesn't foul the cylinder front, and similarly that when the pin is at its furthest point from the cylinder the rod is still located in the cylinder and doesn't come out, thus flopping around and locking up the valve gear, with potentially damaging consequences.

0-4-4 and 4-4-0 locomotives

Locomotives of these wheel arrangements deserve a brief mention because of special problems of balance. Generally speaking, these types of locomotives have considerable overhang over the trailing or leading bogie, which can cause the locomotive to tilt down on the bogie or to drop quite dramatically when setting off bogie first. There are a number of ways of dealing with this, and indeed some kit manufacturers provide quite ingenious mechanical and springing arrangements to overcome this tendency to 'over-balance'.

My arrangement is simplicity itself - crude and simple but nevertheless effective. All that is required is a spring of bent strip or wire fixed to the bogie and bearing on the underside of the loco body between the frames; it needs to be adjusted sufficiently to keep the loco level and prevent dropping or the body being push upward by the spring - a simple question of tweaking. Note that the shorter the length of the leg on the spring, the stiffer the action.

Compensation, equalising or rigid chassis?

There is an increasing tendency towards springing, compensation, equalisation, etc, of wagons, locomotives and, to a lesser extent, bogie coaches. The theory

behind this is twofold. First, it aids running by providing flexibility and helping to keep the wheels on the track despite a modest and inevitable unevenness, particularly at joints, crossing vees, etc. This consequently aids the running of locomotives because there is more chance of all the wheels being on the track at any one time and thus conducting current to the motor. The second element is that it improves the appearance of running as wagons in particular don't jolt over track joints and irregularities.

Undoubtedly both theories are in practice true. The question is whether it is worth the effort, which in some cases is quite considerable because, for example, if you allow vertical movement of the driving wheels of six-coupled locomotives, the rods need to be joined, which is, unless provided for in the kit or rods you are using, a whole new can of worms!

There is no short answer. I have locomotives with rigid, sprung and equalised chassis, and to be honest there is no noticeable difference in performance. My approach, being basically a lazy individual who doesn't like making work, is to incorporate one of these features if the kit provides for it, for example the springing in our '4F', to be discussed later.

Wagons are a different matter and, as we will see in the next chapter, various types have been used, again where provided for in the kit.

I have concluded that on anything like half decent track the bogies on bogie coaches and vehicles can provide enough flexibility not to need any additional provision. However, six-wheel and long-wheelbase four-wheel vehicles are a different matter and the accompanying illustration shows one satisfactory arrangement.

Painting and lining

This is the aspect of modelling technique that can turn an average model into something a bit special - or a good model into a mess. Done properly, it can make a model live with the detail and feel created with a few strokes of the paintbrush. Details of painting and lining wagons, coaches and locomotives are discussed in their respective chapters, but here are a few general observations.

Preparation and materials

I will begin with a look at painting plastic rolling-stock. Most people will say that you need enamel or acrylic paint and that you shouldn't use cellulose car paint as it will damage the plastic. True, but you can use cellulose on plastic providing that you apply light coats. You will in all probability get a slightly mottled effect, some patches being gloss and others matt. However, if you apply enamel varnish afterwards, this will disappear and a perfectly normal surface finish will result.

With plastic-bodied coaches in 4 mm scale I regularly use both acrylic and cellulose car aerosol paint, lining out afterwards in enamel paint. If you use cellulose you must ensure that you don't spray it on enamel or acrylic as it will cause it to blister, so paint the cellulose first, the acrylic or enamel second; for example, a black smokebox on a crimson lake locomotive.

Generally speaking I use aerosol sprays, either special matt enamels for modellers, the colour-matched Rail Match range or car aerosol touch-up cans available in such a variety of colours that one is bound to be suitable for your model: for example, BL Damask Red is a good LMS/BR Crimson Lake.

The key to any paint job is the preparation. The model must be clean and free from dust, grease, imperfections in the surface, gaps between joints, and lumps of excess solder or glue. On plastic models you have to be careful not to scratch the surface and leave marks that will show through the light coat of paint that will be applied. Corners, joints and moulding pips should be carefully cleaned and smoothed with a fine wet and dry paper, and any dust from this process blown away and brushed off with a camera lens brush and blower.

Any filling can be done with Milliput, a two-pack filler putty that needs to be mixed in small quantities. I find it easiest to apply with a small knife - a craft knife is good - enabling you to get in between detail and between corners. When the putty is in place and roughly to shape, it can be finally smoothed by moistening the knife blade and smoothing it over. This putty has only a very slight propensity to shrink on drying, so you only need to leave it very slightly proud

on bigger fillings, finishing it off with the finest wet and dry when thoroughly set and hardened. This filling procedure and the use of Milliput applies exactly the same to plastic, cast metal, brass or aluminium models.

When you have scraped off the excess solder and glue and filled all the gaps, the next stage is to clean the model prior to priming. As has already been said, on plastic models it is simply a matter of blowing and brushing off any dust or debris. This is also necessary on metal models, and we then have to also consider the removal of flux traces on models that have been soldered. On locomotive chassis I will use the burnishing tool after scraping away excess solder, and this is usually sufficient. However, on the loco body, where a good finish is essential, I will immerse it overnight in a bowl of warm water into which has been added a touch of washing-up liquid. The model is then removed and dried thoroughly and washed with lighter fuel to degrease it. *Be very careful as this material is highly flammable. Do not use it on plastic. It will damage the material.* I apply the fuel on a swab of some old absorbent material that doesn't leave fibres behind - a very important consideration. The fuel will evaporate quickly and the model can then be primed.

Almost exclusively I use grey aerosol primer sold for car repairs and have found it to be excellent, particularly at showing up any defects in the surface of the model. Indeed, this is one of the great advantages of priming; not only does it help the top coat paint to stick to the model, it also highlights defects that you cannot see clearly when the model is still in bare plastic or metal.

If the priming process shows gaps, fill them, clean off and prime again, repeating until you are happy with the surface. If the priming shows dust, glue or solder, carefully remove it and blend into the surrounding primer with fine wet and dry, then re-prime. Repeat if necessary until you are happy that you have a blemish-free surface.

Make sure that you apply the primer in quick, light coats until you have an even coverage and no runs. Make sure the primer gets into all the corners and, if you are painting a locomotive, that you prime underneath as well. When you are happy with the surface and finish you can consider the top coat, which we will discuss in more detail later.

3.
FREIGHT STOCK

I am going to start looking at the provision of the necessary locomotives and stock for Platt Lane by considering the goods side of things. This is because the humble goods wagon is probably the most neglected area of modelling and, certainly for most, far less interesting than locomotives and other stock. Indeed, if my thoughts on this aspect were tucked away at the end they would probably not be read!

There is also a very practical reason for starting with wagons - they are generally a good introduction to modelling, whether you are building kits or scratchbuilding. But before we actually start to look at the model wagons it is as well to look at goods trains in the steam era.

Goods trains in the steam era

For the majority of railways the carriage of freight in all its various forms was the most important kind of traffic. The carriage of freight was a complex business and the patterns laid down, and indeed the types of vehicles used, changed little in basic concept from the turn of the century until the 1960s. There were, however, a number of attempts by the railway companies, particularly in the 1930s and '40s and by BR after the mid-'50s Modernisation Plan, to improve practice and increase efficiency to enable them to compete better with the increasing inroads in goods carriage by the motor lorry.

There are a number of common myths about how railways handled freight traffic, and particularly about the vehicles used. In the next few paragraphs I have set out some background using the Great Western Railway as an example (out of sheer laziness - it is much easier to look at the GWR as a continuous entity as it was the least affected of all the railway companies in England by the Grouping of 1923). However,

the picture painted can be generally regarded as typical of all the 'Big Four' railways created in 1923, although the Southern was somewhat different in scale and, with its preponderance of commuter traffic, character.

The first myth to explode is the use of covered vans. It is a fact that on Britain's railways up to the Second World War 90 per cent of wagon stock was open merchandise stock. In 1902 the GWR had 54,161 merchandise wagons, 2,585 loco and coal wagons, 9 loco vans and 2,281 engineers' vehicles. At the Grouping the absorption of vehicles from constituent companies increased the GWR's stock of wagons by approximately 37,000 vehicles. The immediate post-First World War period saw the widespread replacement of older 19th-century vehicles with larger, more modern open wagons and vans and, indeed, much of the absorbed stock was soon condemned, resulting in about 8,000 fewer vehicles in 1926 than in 1923.

The vast majority of wagons in use prior to the Second World War for carrying minerals, particularly coal, coke and iron ore, were privately owned by mines or distributors and merchants. In the early 1930s there was a ratio of 5 to 1 private ownership to railway company ownership of mineral wagons, and, in terms of total wagons in use, in 1938 there were 660,155 private owner wagons to 583,789 railway-owned vehicles. In that year ownership of wagons by the GWR was as follows:

Wagon type	Number in stock
Open wagons	47,385
Covered wagons	27,787
Cattle wagons	3,070
Rail and timber trucks	2,367
Special wagons	2,318
Brake vans	2,311
Mineral wagons	1,215
Total wagons in stock	86,453

Top right Until the 1970s the development of the humble British goods wagon was evolutionary rather than revolutionary. Here is an example of that evolution, the van on the right still showing very clear lineage from the earlier type on the left, but with a new arrangement for the doors to enable easier loading of palletised goods. These later vehicles, a product of the 1960s, are now themselves extinct. This one had an interesting life, being used by the Royal Ordnance, and is seen here saved for preservation at the East Lancashire Railway, Bury. *Author's collection*

Middle right The medium goods wagon, often referred to by modellers as a five-plank wagon. Because of their use as general merchandise vehicles and their greater versatility and better construction when inherited by BR in 1948, these vehicles lasted much longer in traffic than their seven-plank mineral wagon counterparts. This vehicle, seen in Bolton, has its origins on the GWR, as indicated by the running number. BR gave wagons new number series that were prefixed by 'M' for LMS-built vehicles, 'W' for GWR, 'E' for LNER and 'S' for Southern, whereas BR-built vehicles had the prefix 'B'. This view shows clearly the livery details of wooden-bodied vehicles - the grey body work indicates an unfitted vehicle. *D. Hampson*

Bottom right The 16-ton mineral wagon was the direct replacement vehicle for the thousands of wooden-bodied, ex-private owner wagons inherited by BR. It had several variations and in the late 1950s some were fitted with vacuum brakes. However, this was found to foul automatic control equipment and was subsequently removed. These vehicles were ubiquitous in the late 1950s and throughout the '60s and early '70s, forming long trains of similar vehicles snaking from the collieries or fitting snugly in branch-line freights. They are essential for modellers of the BR period up to the 1980s, and provide a good challenge for the modeller who likes well-worn wagons.

The white diagonal stripe on the wagon next to the brake van indicates an end door and, remarkably, seems often to have been the last bit of paint on a thoroughly rusted body. The design, construction and variants of these vehicles has been well documented in the model press and in books on BR wagon development for anyone interested in further study. Here is a train shunting Ashton-in-Makerfield in about 1960. *D. Hampson*

These figures, particularly having regard to the South Wales coal traffic, demonstrate clearly how few mineral wagons were actually owned by the company.

Mineral wagons were very similar in appearance to open merchandise wagons. They carried coal and other minerals (but not loco coal, which was carried, as far as I know, by all major railway companies in Britain in either specially designated or designed and constructed wagons). It is easy on casual observance to confuse mineral and general merchandise wagons, but the former can usually be identified by the drop side doors that do not continue to the top of the side. The inclusion of an end door is also a good indication of a mineral wagon.

Special wagons as a category included vehicles such as creosote or gas oil wagons. The comparatively high number of cattle wagons in the table reflects the importance of this traffic on the GWR and the rural locations, particularly in the West Country, served by the railway. Milk traffic to London was also important and led to the development of the well known 'brown' vehicles for the conveyance of milk churns, and the four- and six-wheeled glass-lined tankers.

Generally, for most railways the main single commodity was coal, the majority of which was carried in 10- and 12-ton private owner wagons, often made up into slow trains of 60 and more vehicles.

Until the establishment of the 'common user' principle in the First World War, railway-owned wagons operating on another company's system had to be returned to the owning company, loaded or not, within five days, or a daily fine would be imposed by the Railway Clearing House (RCH). The 'common user' principle created a pool of unfitted open vehicles and closed merchandise wagons that became interchangeable throughout mainland Britain. This enabled any company's wagon to be loaded and dispatched from anywhere. The number of vehicles agreed for inclusion in this pool by the various companies was determined by reference to the proportion of the freight traffic handled after the Grouping, and was as follows:

Great Western	65,000
LMS	217,000
LNER	170,000
Southern	29,000

Wagons not in the pool were marked accordingly, for example on the GWR: 'Return to GWR - Not Common User'. On the LNER the letter 'N' was painted in the bottom corners of the sides or on the headstocks, and a similar 'N' was placed at the lower edge of the body at each end of non-pool LMS wagons.

You might ask what this has to do with building a model railway. Well, as I said at the outset, goods traffic was essential to the railways, their very life blood. Even casual observers travelling today by train, or looking at land and development, cannot fail to recognise the tracts of land that were once goods yards or sorting sidings, and are now occupied by retail parks, car parks, and even conventional grass parks! Well into the 1960s railways bustled with freight traffic, coal and other merchandise being delivered to goods yards and stations. Indeed, until comparatively recently freight was the main revenue-earner for British Railways.

If freight traffic was important to real railways then it will be important to reflect this on most model railways, and in so doing to reflect the proportions of different types of wagons used by the railways at the era and location of your model railway. As our model, Platt Lane, is set in 1959, well into the British Railways era, we need to take a look at the way wagons developed in this period to help us choose the right type of vehicles for the layout.

Despite the dawn of the brave new world heralded for the railways on their nationalisation in 1948, in reality the new British Railways inherited a rather sad railway system, worn out by the ravages of wartime use with all the short cuts taken to keep the railways running during the emergency and the considerable and excessive usage during that period. Nowhere was this more evident than in the 1,279,543 wagons inherited from the 'Big Four', wagons that had been worked prodigiously and were still carrying, in 1948, truly massive amounts of freight. A large proportion of the wagons in use, up to as many as a third of some of the company's stock inherited, dated back to the pre-Grouping period. Over 70,000 railway-owned wagons were awaiting repair.

The vast majority of vehicles were 'unfitted' (had no continuous automatic brake) with three-link couplings, and were thus suited only to the archetypal British loose-coupled goods train, hardly the basis for a modern railway system geared to the fast movement of freight. The situation was made worse by the still large numbers of wagons with grease-lubricated axle-boxes, which reduced the speed at which they could travel even more, and by the half a million or so private owner wagons used for mineral haulage, requisitioned by the Government at the outbreak of the Second World War. They too became part of the new British Railways stock and, if anything, were in even worse condition than the railway-owned vehicles and generally even more antiquated.

The urgent requirement of the new nationalised railway was to address this situation, something tackled with surprising gusto considering the economic climate of the time. Initially efforts were concentrated

Two variants of basically the same vehicle, the BR standard ventilated van. The vehicle on the left is a planked vehicle but has acquired plywood panelled doors. This type of modification is worth looking at to add some individuality to models. The vehicle on the right is a plywood-sided version of the standard vehicle of which quite a number were built.

These pictures are interesting as they also show the vans in fairly typical condition of the 1960s. *Author's collection*

on repairing the inherited wagons that might thereafter expect a reasonable life expectancy, scrapping those that did not, and replacing them with larger, more modern vehicles, at first to the selected designs of the 'Big Four'. In fact, the earliest new builds were completions of outstanding orders.

Gradually, as the process continued, these designs were altered in detail and eventually new BR designs took over. The new post-nationalisation construction, at least in the beginning, eliminated wooden underframes and grease boxes from new construction and for general traffic vehicles of less than 12 tons capaci-

ty, 16 tons for mineral wagons. It didn't, initially at any rate, greatly increase the number of fitted vehicles. It took the 1955 Modernisation Plan to do this, with a demand for faster 'fitted' trains to meet increasing competition from the roads.

The standard designs prepared for wagons at this juncture will be familiar and will form the basis for some of the wagons we will build for Platt Lane. They were:

10-ton insulated meat van
10-ton ventilated meat van
8-ton cattle wagon
16-ton all steel mineral wagon
24 1/2-ton all-steel mineral wagon
25-ton ironstone wagon
22-ton plate wagon
20-ton goods brake van
13-ton all-steel high-sided goods wagon
12-ton covered goods van
12-ton fruit and vegetable van
8-ton banana van
30-ton bogie bolster
42-ton bogie bolster

Lettering on unfitted BR wagons was generally white on black panels; the latter are easy enough to paint in by hand and, when thoroughly dry, the white lettering can be applied from transfers. There are many types available, but most are the press-fix or self-adhesive types; follow the manufacturers' instructions and be very careful to ensure that the numbers, etc, are straight and, if made up from separately applied numbers, evenly spaced. Don't forget to make sure that your black panels are big enough! The photograph shows three of the Platt Lane vehicles in varying shades of weathering, from the just-washed-over 16-ton mineral wagon to the light weathering of the fitted van, concluding on the right with the battered old ex-Midland wagon.

Liveries

Before we actually move on to look at building the wagons themselves, a few comments on wagon liveries might be appropriate. I will concentrate on the liveries used by BR, as to cover the wagon liveries of the 'Big Four', let alone the pre-Grouping companies, would require a volume on its own. In any event, this aspect is well cov-

ered in various specialist books on pre-nationalisation wagons.

So far as BR is concerned, there were two basic liveries in the pre-TOPS (Total Operations Processing System) period. Unfitted stock was light grey for bodies with black patches on which appeared white lettering. Other markings, such as the stripes to indicate an end door, had no black background. Fitted vehicles had bauxite bodies with white lettering but no black patches.

In both instances, underframes, running gear and solebars were black. However, it seems as if the solebars and headstocks on both fitted and unfitted vehicles were often painted the body colour. In any event, wagons were usually so filthy that it was difficult to tell the colour in which wagons, and particularly their underframes, had been painted!

Open wagons, particularly in the early BR period, were often put into service with the body unpainted save for black patches and lettering and other markings and with black ironwork. It was usual throughout the period for wooden vehicles with patch repairs to have either the replacement plank left unpainted or for there to be patch-painting of repairs rather than the whole wagon repainted.

Departmental or service vehicles were black with yellow lettering, although often service vehicles were down-rated or transferred from general stock and remained in their original colours for many years with perhaps the addition of further markings.

In addition to these basic schemes, there were variations for special vehicles, in particular fitted ones. Insulated and fish vans and containers for these purposes were originally white with black lettering, later becoming blue. Exceptionally, in the early BR period some insulated meat vans had light stone bodies not dissimilar to the Southern Railway scheme, whereas early ventilated meat vans appeared in passenger stock crimson lake with yellow lettering, as did ordinary containers. Both were later to become bauxite. Horse boxes, prize cattle wagons and parcel vans were generally considered as non-passenger coaching stock and are considered in the next chapter.

Goods traffic to Platt Lane

On Platt Lane we need to provide appropriate vehicles for the services and facilities provided. These are basically domestic coal supplies to the coal siding adjacent to the main platforms and general merchandise to Bollings Yard.

Generally speaking, the choice of vehicles will depend upon the period at which the model is set, and as a general rule of thumb the earlier the period,

the more general merchandise will be carried by wagon. Similarly, during the 1950s the ratio of wooden-bodied coal wagons to steel mineral wagons will decrease.

There is no provision for 'special' vehicles such as tank wagons, gunpowder vans, banana vans and china clay wagons, etc, and no special sidings or facilities exist on the layout for these traffics. There is, however, one 'off stage' possibility that could be considered at Platt Lane, which stems from basing the concept of the layout on Bolton Great Moor Street, and this is the location of a brewery, complete with its own siding a mile or so from the station. This local brewery, Magee Marshall & Co, obtained water from Burton-on-Trent and shipped it to its Crown Brewery in Bolton in a fleet of tank wagons, and as far as I am aware this practice was still extant when the brewery was taken over by Greenall Whitley & Co in 1958, but probably didn't last much beyond that. It wasn't technically necessary to brew beer with water from Burton, and part of the explanation may lie in the fact that Magee Marshall had owned a brewery in Burton-on-Trent. Indeed, the Railway Clearing House handbook for 1904 shows that there were sidings belonging to Magee Marshall at Bolton, Burton and Castleton (Rochdale).

By the time of our model the water was obtained from the Burton Pure Ice & Water Company. The wagons came from Burton-on-Trent via Crewe and Warrington and arrived at Crook Street goods depot, which is where Bollings Yard would be on Platt Lane. The wagons were then worked to the brewery siding, which was shunted as often as five times a week. Wagons were commonly dispatched and received two at a time, rather than in less frequent but longer train loads.

The brewery had large storage tanks into which the water was pumped via a water main that ran between the rails of the siding. While at the sidings the tank wagons were swilled out and the inside paintwork patched if needed; local folklore has it that it was not uncommon for disgruntled employees and others to relive themselves in the water - perhaps it was this rather than the Burton water that gave the beer its flavour?

The company operated a variety of wagons, the earliest in use in the 1950s dating from 1908. Many of them were rectangular or 'rectanks' of similar overall appearance, the difference usually relating to size and location of manholes and valves. The livery of these vehicles was deep maroon for the chassis and underframe with white lettering and RCH insignia in yellow. There were also four conventional cylindrical tanks of 3,000-gallon capacity, with welded tanks, and a further riveted cylindrical tank example that had an

Magee Marshall 'rectank' wagon No 8 built in 1934. This is the only picture I have seen of one of these vehicles in service and is alas unfortunately not very good. I have detailed their use in the text and you have to take my word for it that a very acceptable model could be adapted from a standard 'rectank' kit to suit a specific local application. *Author's collection*

unusual brake gear, possibly of the Dean Churchward type? The cylindrical tanks were built in 1947, except for the last-mentioned example, which had been built 20 years earlier.

It is possible to assume with our model that there is a brewery siding 'off stage' and that the wagons are brought in to Bollings Yard as part of a shunt process, then 'cut out' and sent by 'trip' working to the brewery. It adds a further dimension to the operation of the model and is based on reality rather than a pure figment of imagination. Who knows, one day the layout may even be extended to include an 'on stage' section with a brewery siding.

The type of coal facilities available on the layout, coal drops, also

Above right A 'Jinty' heading a typical 'trip' working comprising a quantity and variety of wagons that could be accommodated at Platt Lane. *D. Hampson*

Right A view typical of mineral trains in the area and period being modelled on the project layout. Note the variety of wagons as late as 1961 when this shot was taken at Kearsley. *D. Hampson*

has a bearing on the types of vehicle used to bring in the coal; bottom-door or hopper wagons would be the preferred option. Notice that I hedge my bets on this, because as with many things railway, what should be a logical deduction, a near certainty in reality, may not always be. I remember seeing principally 16-ton steel mineral wagons and 21-ton hoppers at Great Moor Street, long after closure to passengers, but also the 21-ton steel mineral wagons that did not have bottom doors. I can only assume the door flaps were dropped and somehow the coal shovelled out to fall down the shutes, something I would have thought unlikely.

In the early 1950s the mineral wagons would primarily be wooden ex-private owner, bottom-door vehicles, with perhaps an odd early type of steel wagon. By 1960 there would be few wooden-bodied wagons, the make-up having reversed. Prior to nationalisation they would have been private owners' vehicles, of which there are a great many on the market in the popular modelling scales either ready to run or in kits. However, you should be a little more discriminating than just going for the nice bright red one with standard white lettering, or the one whose name you haven't got!

Broadly, private owner mineral wagons fall into two categories, mine or quarry owners and merchants or

distributors. If you are modelling the pre-BR period, you will need to have cognisance of the ownership of private owner vehicles in the area in which your model is set. Prime candidates for Platt Lane would be Hulton Colliery wagons. So far as I am aware, no ready-to-run or pre-lettered kits exist of Hulton Colliery vehicles, but the name could be created from transfers. The wagons used by private owners would be bought from outside manufactures, and would need to comply to RCH specifications.

A word of caution on private owner wagons. They might look very pretty in their colours with bright lettering, but if you look at photographs they did not retain this brightness for long in traffic. The very use of a vehicle on a steam railway soon took care of that. Add to that loading, often from hoppers or above the vehicle, and unloading in colliery and coal sidings and you get the picture. The bright, bold lettering was no doubt needed to stand a chance of still proclaiming ownership after a year or two in service!

So far as the general merchandise is concerned, as we have seen the earlier your model is set, the less common was the use of vans. In fact, even in 1930 far more general merchandise was carried in sheeted open

BR built large quantities of brake vans with a central cabin and open platforms at either end, based on an LNER design. These are few in number now and confined to departmental use, where there are also some LMS-design vans of the fitted type illustrated here. Bolton yard, 1960. *D. Hampson*

wagons than in vans. However, this situation rapidly changed during the 1930s through to the 1950s, with increasing numbers of vans being built - mind you it took until 1971 before vans outnumbered wagons!

Left A northbound Scots goods leaving Entwistle, between Bolton and Blackburn. This fitted freight is interesting for the container traffic it contains, a type of conveyance heavily promoted in the 1950s and '60s but rarely modelled. You don't, by the way, need a 'Conflat' to carry your container - a fitted low-sided open wagon was also used. *D. Hampson*

Below left Not all goods trains comprised large engines and 40 or 50 wagons. There was quite a variety, in fact so much so that beyond the rules of train composition and marshalling there was little chance of standardisation save for the long coal trains or special van trains of the 1960s. There is also plenty of evidence, particularly at the twilight of steam, of some unusual motive power being used, such as 'Jubilees' and 'Royal Scots' on local freights, and 'Coronation' 'Pacifics' on fitted freights. This view shows a large 'WD' 2-8-0 with what can only be described as a minimalist train. *D. Hampson*

One type of wagon not yet considered, but as essential as the locomotive before the days of air-braked trains, is the brake van. This performed the vital function of helping to control the train. Remember that the majority of vehicles and thus whole goods trains were unfitted; they did not have a continuous brake of any kind that could be operated from the locomotive. In this scenario, the importance of the goods guard cannot be over-emphasised. He was a key man in the movement of freight, he needed to know the road and needed to be able to anticipate the driver's requirement to prevent the train from taking control, particularly on downhill gradients.

Being located at the very rear of the train, the brake van displayed lamps that provided an essential means of communication to signalmen and crews of trains on adjacent lines. Lamp positions varied according to the usage of the train, not, like loco headlamps, with the train type or route.

Brake vans had been built in a variety of sizes, or rather weights, but by the 1920s it was commonly accepted that anything less than 20 tons was not going to be much use at stopping trains. While prior to nationalisation brake vans were usually operated within their own systems, some vans even being labelled for special routes, services or depots, in BR days there was some movement beyond this old system. The ex-Southern Railway 'pill box' type could, for example, be seen occasionally in the North West, making a contrast to the LMS and BR designs; however, I don't recall seeing any ex-GWR 'Toads'! BR itself built large numbers of vans, and together with the later ex-LMS designs, these seem to have outlived others.

I have set out in the accompanying table a suggestion for the make-up of wagon stock for Platt Lane at three different periods. The numbers are arbitrary - it is the type that is of more concern, and the balance between the types.

---

1. 1912, LNWR period

Type	Quantity
Private owner coal wagons	20
Private owner open wagons (five-plank mineral)	2
General merchandise wagons (open, company-owned)	10 (5 LNWR, 5 other companies)
Covered vans	2 (1 LNWR and 1 Midland or L&Y)
Low-sided wagons (company-owned)	1
Brake vans (LNWR)	4

2. 1933, LMS period

Private owner coal wagons	20
Private owner mineral wagons (five-plank)	2
Covered vans	5 (1 LNER, 2 LMS standard, 2 pre-Grouping constituents)
General merchandise wagons (open)	8 (5 LMS, 3 other companies)
Low-sided wagons (LMS)	1
Brake vans (LMS)	4 (1 pre-Grouping, 3 LMS types)

3. 1950, BR period

Wooden-bodied coal wagons (ex-PO)	17
Steel-bodied coal wagons (16-ton)	2
General merchandise wagons (open)	4 (3 LMS standard 1923 design and 1 other)
Covered vans	8 (1 fitted)
Low-sided wagons	3 (1 five-plank, 1 three-plank, 1 'Conflat')
Brake vans	4 (3 later LMS standard type, 1 earlier type)

4. 1959, BR period

Wooden-bodied coal wagons (ex-PO)	4
Steel-bodied wagons	8 (7 16-ton mineral wagons, 1 21-ton wagon)
Steel 21-ton hoppers	6
General merchandise wagons	3 (1 wooden 'High Bar', 2 steel-bodied)
Covered vans	10 (8 fitted, 2 unfitted)
Low-sided wagons	3 (2 'Conflats', 1 'Lowfit')
Brake vans	4 (2 LMS, 2 BR standard)

As many as 39 wagons may seem an excessive number, but it is not the total quantity that is important, rather the type and their ratio. Thirty-nine wagons would swamp Platt Lane, which is after all a comparatively small O gauge layout, and I would not want to see all the siding space crammed with wagons, something that would not be all that appropriate for 1959 and, perhaps more importantly, something that, even if it were correct, would be visually jarring. If you don't believe me, try filling your siding space, then look at it. Compromise is necessary, and I think you will be the best judge, within the overall parameters of prototype practice. This concept of reality looking 'wrong' is rather interesting, and is something we will come to again.

Modelling freight stock

The types of wagons outlined in the table are straightforward acquisitions for a model railway as kits or ready to run items in most of the common scales. As we are primarily addressing O gauge, I will concentrate on producing the vehicles from kits, but as the same materials are used to produce kits in 4 and 7 mm scales, the techniques for building them will generally be equally applicable.

The wagon kits available to modellers are generally from plastic, white metal, etched brass or, particularly in O gauge, a combination of materials. There is, however, one example of an RCH 1923 mineral wagon that actually features a wooden-planked body!

If you haven't much experience or much success at building kits, wagons are a good place to start, being relatively inexpensive; also, because of their usually less than pristine condition, botches and mistakes can often be disguised. In fact, if the worst happens you can always park it at the end of a siding somewhere, condemned and rotting away, or use the body as some form of grounded shed or adjunct to a farmyard!

Assembly notes and instructions vary enormously from kit to kit, from several pages of notes to a sketch and a few notes. However, despite assembly instructions being the source of some ridicule in modelling circles, they are a good place to start your preparation, as the manufacturer may have designed into his product some peculiarity or feature that limits the vehicle to a specific batch and thus modification may be necessary, or there may be a particular construction sequence that it is necessary to follow to complete the kit.

Van roofs, sometimes floors where provided, are often plastic. These can be fixed in place with 'superglue' or sparing use of contact adhesive on metal models. Roofs may well be just a flat piece of plastic, with the builder being left to cut and shape it and add detail such as rain strips and ventilators.

I always think it is essential to get a well-fitting roof, clean and well detailed, as it is the most visible part of the wagon when on the layout. I don't think this can be achieved by simply sticking the plastic on the body and hoping that it will retain its shape and neatness by gluing it to the edges.

Accordingly I always pre-curve the roof to the correct shape and build a subframe to the profile of the ends that slots into the inside of the body with the roof overhanging as appropriate.

After plastic perhaps the most common material for wagon kits is white metal. The basic tool kit of knife, files and abrasive paper is supplemented by 'superglue' for assembling castings and perhaps a low-voltage soldering iron and low-melt solder. As with plastic kits, construction usually begins with the underframe and running gear. Care needs to be taken to ensure that the underframe is square, and a plate glass base on which to work is essential. Soldering can be a bit fiddly, and as you have to ensure that no movement of the piece takes place prior to the solder cooling to solid, various pins, blocks and hairclips can be pressed into service to avoid too much damage to the fingers!

Similar care needs to be taken in aligning brake gear with the wheels, but if you do need to pack or space any components and you are soldering, remember to choose your packing material carefully, ie something that will not melt while you are soldering in adjacent areas!

White metal is relatively heavy, so when handling the vehicle during construction be careful not to risk picking it up or moving it by one of the more delicate parts. They can easily break and the heavier main construction fall to the work bench or, worse still, the floor, with disastrous results - I know, I have done it!

Invariably, etched kits will require the metal to be bent. The general rule is that the half-etched lines, best identified as a channel in the metal, are on the *inside* of any fold or bend, ensuring that the bend is as sharp as possible and square. Some assistance with the bend is essential; bending bars are ideal, but improvisation with steel bar and blocks of hardwood can help. Simple bending bars are two long strips of thin metal of equal size, riveted together at each end. The component to be bent is slid between the two bars and, with the aid of a further flat surface, the metal can be bent.

For small components such as brackets or brake hangers, bends of 90 degrees can be achieved best by using long-nose pliers. Be warned, however, that you need good-quality pliers with a close accurate action that will not wander and thus prevent a good clean hold and therefore a correspondingly good bend.

Etched kits are definitely not quickie kits, but the level of detail and strength of the finished model, the crispness of detail and thinness of components and edges, can be well worth the effort.

Right There are a few pre-liminaries necessary before we can begin constructing a model wagon. The first and most obvious is to choose the appropriate types for the layout, and select the appropriate kits. The second is to decide, having looked at the kit, whether you want to modify it in any way, add detail or improve it by, say, providing interior planking and bolt detail to open wagons if the kit does not show this detail. If you are going to make any of these amendments, it is essential to plan for them, not least for ease of accomplishment. It is quite straightforward to score planking lines on the inside of a side prior to assembly, but nigh on impossible when you have made the wagon up!

It is also useful to know before you begin what the livery is to be and whether there is any need to plan for this in the construction; for example, if it is a brake van the roof might need to be removable to get at the interior. Or it may be advisable to make the vehicle in separate assemblies, brought together after painting to facilitate a complex paint scheme or lining. It is unlikely that any of the instructions or assembly notes provided will cover these possibilities.

Here we see the addition of planking and bolt detail on the inside of a wagon. It is essential to make sure that the lines on the inside correspond to the planking on the outside! I prefer to mark the internal plank lines from the top downwards, because if I make a mistake and the distance does not work out, it is less noticeable if the discrepancy is at the bottom.

There are a couple of ways of representing bolt-heads. One is to 'punch' them out of thin plasticard, 10 or 15 thou, using a short length of 1 mm square metal, another is to slice off thin tranches of appropriate section plasticard strip. However, the best and easiest method is to use ready-manufactured bolt-head detail, readily available in the USA, and in the UK from specialist suppliers. The key thing is to apply the detail in the correct position in relation to the outside detail.

Left You also need to be careful that what you represent on the inside mirrors not only the external provision but also the function of the vehicle. Contrast, for example, the planking arrangement of the previous picture, which represents a simple side-door wagon, with that shown here, which has bottom and side doors. Consequently the bottom door needs to be reflected in the planking, which is just about visible in this picture.

Right There was a time when manufacturers made virtually everything from the materials in which they specialised, leading to some parts not being made from necessarily the best materials; for example, plastic buffers and complex fabrications might be made from layers of etched brass sweated together to give a shape that would better be reproduced as a casting or moulding. The current tendency, however, is for a composite kit or one made from several materials using those most appropriate to the job. This manifests itself in steel buffers and detailed castings such as the stove in the brake van interior shown here.

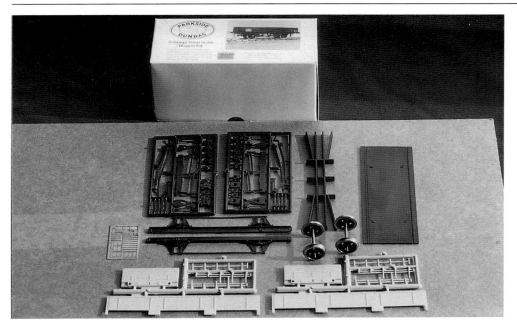

Top left Typical components of a plastic wagon kit, the Parkside Dundas 'Grampus' ballast wagon. This illustrates the use of a variety of materials - etched brass joins plastic and white metal castings to give some of the finer detail.

Middle left In most cases the usual place to commence construction proper is with the wagon underframe. In the case of this Parkside Dundas van, the underframe is built on to the floor, but as the van body ends contain the headstock and the van chassis needs to fit between this, the body was assembled first.

Invariably plastic wagon bodies are built around a floor, which forms a base for the construction of the underframe. Whatever the wagon, a square assembly and neat corner joints are essential, as are careful preparation and cleaning of the parts. Flash and moulding 'pips' should be carefully removed, then the components offered together in a dry assembly until the best fit is achieved. It is well worthwhile to double-check that the body will fit round the floor prior to assembling the chassis to avoid the risk of damage to the delicate underframe parts by having to trim down the floor later.

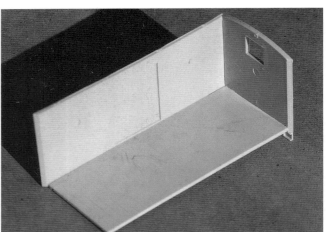

Even if you are adopting compensation for your wagon stock, you need to take care to ensure that the assembly is square. I still find, despite all sorts of complicated jigs that have been devised over the years, that there is no substitute for a piece of glass as a level surface on which to begin construction. It is worthwhile allowing the basic assembly to set thoroughly before applying detail, thus avoiding the risk of disturbing it when adding detail parts.

Bottom left Most plastic wagon kits, at least in 7 mm scale, come complete with wheels. The question of compensation for wagons, and indeed coaches and locomotives, has been debated at length in the modelling press for quite a few years, and now in all the popular scales and gauges many ingenious methods have been devised. In some kits vertical movement is achieved by the simple expedient of allowing a degree of free vertical movement of the axleboxes in the 'W' irons. Other perhaps more common methods usually incorporate some form of movement of the whole 'W' iron, which is etched in brass and allows one axle to pivot on a central fulcrum while the other remains fixed, as seen here.

The axles are turned to a point and run in turned brass bearing cups, which are pushed into holes moulded in the axlebox. Don't forget these important matters. I have picked up wagons only to find that the builder has omitted to fit them and can't understand why at best its motion is wobbly.

Here you can see the principle of the movement of the axleboxes in the 'W' irons: the box on the left is higher in the iron than the one on the right, which is at the lower limit of its travel. It is essential that these axleboxes move freely up and down to enable free movement of the wheels to respond to the ups and downs of the track.

It is sometimes necessary to pack the components carrying the brake shoes, lifting them a little from the floor to ensure that the shoes match the wheels; usually the centre of the shoe is in line with the wheel centre. This is often all that is necessary to avoid the shoe touching the wheel and acting as a real brake. If there is a lot of side play in the wheel sets, it is quite easy to reduce this by placing fibre washers between the wheel and the inside of the axlebox. This also helps to avoid the shoes rubbing on the wheel and allows the shoe to be as close as possible for realism. Side play is not usually an issue on four-wheel goods vehicles, and in fact its limitation can help reduce the chances of buffer-locking on sharply curved sidings or reverse curves, as it restricts the outward swing of the extremities of the body - only marginally, I admit, but every little helps. This view shows the completed van underframe.

One of the simplest of detail improvements is the replacement of moulded detail such as handrails and handles with separately applied wire ones. However, even this simple modification is best done before the assembly of the vehicle sides.

The moulded detail requires very careful removal with a sharp knife to avoid damage to the surrounding areas. If there is a complex moulded detail mounting for a stanchion or handle, you may wish to keep it and merely remove the moulded representation of the handle or handrail.

I have always found that it pays to measure very carefully the length of the handrail and drill out holes for the wire. Bend the wire at 90 degrees or as appropriate to fix it in the hole. Try to make the bend crisp and square, best accomplished by bending the wire around fine-nose pliers and pushing the short leg down tightly with the plain end of a heavy file or similar object.

The completed wagon, ready for the paint shop. Where possible, when steel-turned buffer heads and shanks are provided, I do not fix these on the model until after painting, as nothing looks better on the shanks than polished steel. It is easy to paint the buffer heads after assembly. This also avoids paint clogging up the buffers and reducing springing.

Painting freight stock

The painting and finishing of goods stock is an easy enough task. I will emphasise again that time spent ensuring a good surface to take the paint is time well spent. Clearly, livery details should be established before the painting is commenced. I generally spray-paint wagon underframes using a matt black aerosol model enamel or car touch-up, applying several light coats rather than trying to cover in one or two heavy ones. If possible split the body from the chassis for painting, but don't worry if you can't, as it is a simple matter to mask the wagon body with paper and masking tape while painting the chassis. I will normally also try and remove the wheels or at least mask the wheel treads and flanges - strips of masking tape will do.

As mentioned in the previous chapter, it is essential to remove any traces of flux and excess solder from metal kits before painting, and use of a fibreglass burnishing tool will help to ensure a smooth, even surface. Use sight and feel to establish the finish, and when you are happy with it an application of cigarette lighter fuel on a cotton pad will clean off any final traces of grease. *Be careful with this fluid as it is highly inflammable and its fumes are dangerous if breathed in a confined space for any length of time.*

Prime any metal kits with car aerosol touch-up paint primer before painting the top coat. When this has thoroughly dried it will show up any imperfections that could not be seen beforehand. These should be treated and a further coat of primer applied before the top coat.

Car aerosol paints are very useful and the primers

give a nice matt, mid-grey or bauxite colour to wagon bodies. The gloss colours in the touch-up range are so vast in colour and shade that often the colour you need for your model is available. They are also useful for coaches (of which more later) as well as vans and passenger-rated vehicles such as horse boxes, which often had a finish matching contemporary coaching stock. They are an alternative to specially matched spray paints and usually available at the local car spares shop on a Sunday!

Spray paints require the application of several light coats, allowing a good hour between coats to build up a finish. The car sprays dry very quickly, and produce a very hard finish after a few days, on which lining can be carried out or further details applied with enamel paints. If a mistake is made, the enamel can easily be removed without damaging the cellulose surface of the main body colour below.

For wagon bodies in 4 mm scale (except passenger-rated vehicles, which are finished similarly to coaches) and open wagons in 7 mm scale, I brush paint. The secret is to use a good-quality brush, a lot larger than you will think appropriate, size 4 for 4 mm, size 6 for 7 mm, and apply new paint, thinned and well stirred, taking two or sometimes three coats. I always use matt paints for wagons, as a wagon with a high gloss surface just does not look right on a model, except for vehicles finished in passenger liveries. Allow overnight drying between coats, placing the model in a spacious, clean box to protect it from any dust that will affect the finish. Airbrushing, if you have one, is obviously a most acceptable way of finishing wagons and particularly useful if a batch of vehicles is to be painted at one time.

If individuality can be added easily by adding or leaving out parts of the kit, then it can just as easily be added with paint. As already noted, goods wagons worked hard for their living and even in the golden age of railways, before the First World War, when locos and coaches were immaculately turned out, wagons were not being subjected to the rigours of cleaners.

Weathering and dirtying locomotives and stock is a much debated topic amongst railway modellers in Great Britain, but it is normal practice in the USA where the standards of realism achieved are quite fantastic. It is my view that, particularly with goods stock, a weathered finish on most vehicles is an integral part of creating realistic stock on a working layout and should be carried out. It is all part of the elusive picture we are trying to create.

The basic ingredient in weathering wagons, or making them look used, is observation. At its most basic, the process may simply be the representation of limewash seeping and splashing through cattle wagon sides from the inside. At its most complex, it is an artistic masterpiece where every aspect is covered, down to the splits and chavels in woodwork.

Conveniently and rather simplistically, weathering can be categorised as:

1 The overall film of dirt any object acquires when left outside, and fading due to weather.

2 The dirt and stains caused by the use of the vehicle, for example coal dust or sand.

3 Rust on exposed metal such as running gear, bolt-heads, etc.

4 Deposits from brake fittings around the underframe.

5 Special details such as the aforementioned limewash stains on cattle wagons, spillage around tank fillers on oil tank wagons, or grease marks around axleboxes and other moving parts such as brake lever pivots.

This list also represents a convenient order for the weathering process that you can carry out to

Below As wagons rarely get a wash, they soon aquire a coat of dirt and discoloration, bearing little resemblance to a livery. In addition we can represent repairs of wagon planks, which often remained unpainted, and the effects of the traffic they were used for, such as china clay dust on a vehicle. Here is a well-weathered seven-plank coal wagon, which not only reflects the replacement of planks but faintly betrays its private owner origins beneath the grey BR livery and the ravages of time - just!

Bottom Be careful how you bring your vehicles to life, however. I spent considerable effort on detailing, painting and weathering a cattle wagon, even to the representation of splashes of the limewash to the outside of the vehicle (limewash was used on the wagon interiors to keep down the risk of infection). However, my wagon was in BR livery and at one exhibition a visitor pointed out to me that the practice of limewashing cattle wagon interiors was not carried on after nationalisation! This was something that had never occurred to me to check, as I had assumed the practice continued - it's true what they say about the word assume making an ASS out of U and ME.

This view of an LNER 'J39' near York with a loaded cattle train shows again the point made earlier in the book about loaded cattle wagons being coupled behind the tender. The train has a mixed bunch of mainly BR standard and ex-LNER fitted vehicles, and there is no evidence of limewash. . . *Author's collection*

whatever degree you consider appropriate. Remember that wagons don't weather equally, so each one should be treated to varying degrees. If you model the contemporary scene, take a look at the real thing. Some ideas can be gained from photographs in specialised wagon books for earlier periods.

Obviously the first step is to paint and finish the wagon, including lettering, as if it were new. When this is dry, the overall grime colour is applied. Here an airbrush, while useful, is not an essential - a large, quality brush and a wash of well-stirred and thinned matt paint will do. The choice of colour is obviously a matter of your own preference and observation. I use a dark, dirty brown-grey from the Humbrol range, No 66, and vary its shade slightly by the addition of a little matt white or matt black to lighten or darken respectively. I also use a varied consistency for the wash, adding more or less thinners for particular vehicles. The greater the number of washes, the greater the colour density achieved.

The second stage is the addition of the 'coloration of use'. Clearly the colour used here will depend on the load the vehicle carries, for example black for coal, milk/off-white for china clay, etc. A study of pictures of the vehicles concerned will give an indication of where this weathering should be applied. There are plenty of photographs in specialist books that show up easily the effect on china clay wagons. although black coal dust is not as easily discernable in black and white photographs; however, the Jane's colour albums provide a good reference source.

A different technique is called for in applying the paint at this stage, and that is 'dry brushing'. This is a simple technique whereby a brush loaded with an appropriate colour has the paint wiped from it; the brush will still retain some remnants of paint, which would only be removed by washing in thinner, and it is these remnants that are required on the model. Rubbing the now nearly empty brush across the chosen part of the model will leave this paint in uneven streaks, particularly on raised detail. With practice a considerable and useful variety of finishes can be achieved with dry brushing, the continued use of which can build up the finish to the level you require. A similar process, but stippling the surface with the brush (a round stencil brush is ideal), can also be an effective way of providing particular effects such as rust on a steel-bodied mineral wagon.

The third stage, adding rust to steelwork, can be done with a combination of wash and dry brushing. For a wagon newly in service following a repaint, the brake gear and rigging can be given a light wash of rust colour. Similarly, a slight dry brushing of rust on the body ironwork, such as the bolt-heads and strapping and hinges, can be very effective in helping to depict a well-used wagon. Be careful, however, not to overdo it - as with all weathering, subtlety is the key to success.

The fourth stage is to add track colour, dry brushed again. Only a little is needed, around the brake shoes. Small amounts of gloss black around the axleboxes can hint at old grease and oil deposits.

Last comes the addition of speciality weathering such as the previously mentioned limewash on cattle wagons, and oil spillage around the filler caps of oil tank wagons. The former is represented by liberally splashing the interior, particularly the floor and lower body sides, with a matt off-white, which is allowed to spill to the outside of the lower body and over the underframe. If you can't get into the body for this, dry brush a similar colour on the outside. This will probably be necessary anyway to supplement the first method and achieve anything but a very light coating. Gloss black is carefully applied around and streaked down the side of oil tanks to represent spillage from filling.

Two further touches of individuality can be added. It was common practice to patch and repair wooden-bodied wagons, and particularly in the post-war period for the replacement planking not to be painted. Individual planks can be picked out in a pale grey/buff colour to represent this.

Steel-bodied mineral wagons such as the ubiquitous BR 16-tonner are often seen very heavily rusted, and if you want an authentic-looking train composed of these vehicles, typically it would range from an odd very clean example, almost new looking, through various stages of rusting and toning down of paintwork by the weather, to an odd one that is almost totally rust-covered. This is easily achieved, and the basic toning down and weathering has already been described.

The rust on the body needs some special treatment, however. A combination of dry brushing and stippling of the body with rust paint is required, the shade of which is changed repeatedly but subtly by adding track colour and/or matt black. For some reason, even in badly rusted bodies the white diagonal stripe indicating the end door seems to survive pretty well intact, but in badly rusted wagons takes an orange-coloured staining.

It is possible to achieve the crazed flaking effect of the rust by using cellulose paint on top of enamel base coats, but great care is needed to avoid damage to the plastic body. Dry brushing matt black into the rust - sparingly - will indicate coal dust that has been deposited.

4.
CONVEYING THE PASSENGERS

In pure economic and revenue-earning terms the passenger services operated by the railways were in most cases secondary to the haulage of goods. However, passenger coaches were very important in giving an indication of ownership and origin, and often the type of service for which they were being used.

As with locomotives, and to a lesser extent wagons, the coaching stock was developed with styles and features peculiar to the railway company that built it and to the use for which it was designed. I ought also to mention that many non-passenger-carrying vehicles were also regarded by the railway companies, even British Railways, as coaching stock rather than goods vehicles, although some were included in fitted freight trains. This category of vehicle would include horse boxes, luggage vans, covered combination trucks (CCT), prize cattle vans, motor car trucks, scenery, milk and fish vans.

Despite Platt Lane being set in the late 1950s, the types of vehicles that may typically have been seen in trains of the type we need and in the area being modelled would still contain pre-Grouping rather than purely British Railways standard vehicles, which one might have expected to have permeated local and semi-fast services. Certainly the make-up of trains would be anything but uniform, and would not comprise nice neat sets of similar vehicles. The line being modelled has a clear LNWR origin, and this origin will largely govern the pattern and type of services, but with other appropriate stock still extant from all the pre-Grouping companies, the LNWR would not be the sole provider; but more of this later.

Coaching stock developments

By way of background I thought it would be useful to start with a brief and very simplified outline of coaching stock development and usage on the LNWR and its successor, the LMS. For completeness I have also referred very briefly at the end of this section to BR developments in this area. I emphasise that these are very brief 'potted' histories, and anyone interested in further detail on this very interesting area of railway activity can do worse than to refer to the many specialist books available.

Right, on with the coach development story. The LNWR was billed, or rather billed itself, as the Premier Line, but its billing hardly applied to its coaching stock, which fell way behind that of its chief rival, the Midland (the latter company, incidentally, billed itself as the 'Best Way' until the early years of the present century). While the LNWR brought into service the first corridor train in 1880 (although the vehicles were not of the side-corridor type, a development that the LNWR introduced in 1893), it was still primarily a four- and six-wheel coaching stock railway until the advent of the 42-foot radial coaches on the Webb-designed underframe in the 1880s. These, though, were not bogie coaches, but had the inner two axles fixed, the outermost running in radial trucks - strictly speaking they were eight-wheel coaches! Despite their eccentricity, these vehicles did establish the livery and characteristic design of body panelling and the 'arc roof' style.

By the 1890s the body length of LNWR coaches was generally 28 feet for four-wheel vehicles, 30 feet for a six-wheel vehicles and, after a brief dalliance with 45-foot types, 50 feet for bogie vehicles on 8-foot wheelbase bogies. The LNWR continued to build four- and six-wheel vehicles until the turn of the century and, indeed, built a special set of 11 six-wheel coaches for the Birmingham and Sutton Coldfield services with elliptical roofs as late as 1911, and some four-wheel vehicles were built during 1910/11 for North London Railway services.

By 1893, the best express trains were of 42-foot lavatory stock, although in the same year 42-foot

One of the key parcel vehicles for Platt Lane is the ex-LNWR Diagram 382. Because it has few windows this type of vehicle needs no interior and is often, particularly if you model the post-nationalisation period, anything but pristine, a good introduction to coach building from kits. Here are photographs of the vehicle in LNWR and BR liveries. Built in 1906, they lasted until the early 1960s. Isn't LNWR livery attractive? Both models are from the same Chowbent Castings kit.

the Euston-Liverpool American boat trains and the 2 pm Corridor to Glasgow, complete trains rather than just dining and sleeping cars only.

Even though there were these special sets of coaches built for certain trains, the majority of corridor trains on the LNWR were formed of standard corridor stock. These trains were of little set pattern, giving rise to the very uneven, almost haphazard, appearance of LNWR corridor trains seen in photographs that show trains composed of a variety of lengths and roof styles.

bogie corridor stock trains were introduced, showing the way forward. The length of the vehicles to which I keep referring might seem a bit irrelevant or technical, but I will explain the significance later.

By 1903 the LNWR had made considerable progress in carriage design and had produced many new bogie coaches, dining cars and sleepers, which, in my opinion, were the archetypal Edwardian vehicles. In the period up to the First World War there were further developments that would change the appearance of carriages, with a move from the arc roof to the more modern low elliptical, often described as 'cove', roof, a slightly wider body and 9-foot wheelbase bogies with all-steel coach underframes. Coaches did, however, continue to be built with other dimensions.

As there was less need at this period for new non-corridor stock, these changes were less obvious in those vehicles, although they were usually incorporated in new building. Other developments in the pre-1911 period were primarily the adoption around 1908 of the full elliptical roof and 12-wheeled vehicles for

This is not to say, however, that the LNWR had no method to marshalling its trains, but rather that they were marshalled on the basis of use and need rather than standardisation of styles. This was not peculiar to the LNWR, and modellers should note that trains made up of standard sets and styles were the exception rather than the norm. Indeed, when we consider subsequently the development of passenger trains in the LMS and BR period we will see that it was not until the 1960s that anything like standardisation of vehicle styles was common in train formations, and this was largely as a result of the wholesale scrapping of older vehicles leaving largely, but not exclusively, later pre-nationalisation and British Railways standard vehicles from which to make up trains.

There were of course standard practices, for example the use of specifically labelled sets that could be strengthened by adding additional vehicles, even dining cars, or by simply coupling two sets together, perhaps with a dining car in between or other strengthening vehicles.

Sets, known as inter-corridor sets, normally comprising two Brake 3rds and two Composites, were quite common, but the important point is that the vehicles would not be of the same styles. Individual coaches were replaced and substituted as necessary for repairs, as a result of withdrawal or whatever, rather than complete sets. Looking at photographs of this period the Brake 3rds tend to be of earlier designs than the composites. A typical formation of this type of train, until well into the LMS period might be a Brake 3rd to Diagram 312, two 57-foot 'Toplight' Composites to Diagram 131 and a Brake 3rd to Diagram 314. Later amendments to this type of working are discussed later. Through coach working was catered for by a Brake Composite, but where this was insufficient two-coach sets of Brake 3rd and Composite, effectively half of the inter-district sets, were commonly used.

When it comes to non-corridor stock there are two basic types, lavatory stock and what has commonly become known as 'suburban' stock. The former was, before the widespread introduction of corridor stock, the mainstay of trains travelling any distance, and while built during most periods of LNWR coach construction the majority were of the arc roof type. Furthermore, despite the introduction of corridor stock apparently rendering them obsolete, they were long lived. They were also predominately composite vehicles and were built in all the 'standard' coach lengths. The LNWR also created the 'Inter District Lavatory set', which, usually of three or four coaches maximum, was for journeys of medium duration and was of the cove roof period, being built from 1905.

The standard non-corridor, non-lavatory 'suburban'-type coach was by far the most common, being seen across the system on truly 'suburban' commuter trains in the urban settings of the conurbations and the large towns, as well as rural branch lines. Indeed, they formed the biggest single 'type' of vehicle inherited by the LMS from the LNWR, comprising half of the vehicles so transferred. They were vehicles with little in the way of frills, their prime purpose being to move the maximum number of people. The majority of these vehicles were six-wheelers until about the turn of the century. Even at the

Grouping in 1923 the bulk of those becoming LMS vehicles were arc roof types.

Whilst there were small numbers of shorter bogie vehicles, 42-foot former radial coaches mounted on bogies and 45-foot vehicles, the vast majority of arc roof bogie 'suburban' vehicles were of 50 feet length. There were even some 28-foot and 30-foot arc roof six-wheelers made into bogie vehicles 56 feet and 60 feet long respectively. Examples of 'suburban' vehicles were built in all roof styles and with a gradual increase in length to 57 feet by the end of the LNWR period.

The composition of non-corridor trains was far more 'standard' and neat in appearance than was the case for the corridor trains. This was primarily due to the construction of stock for specific services and the more effective use of time and easier handling of trains composed of set formations. As noted earlier, inter-district sets of between two and four vehicles were the basis of many trains and were usually composed of Brake 3rds and Composites, either suburban or lavatory types depending on the service. It was quite possible, however, for perhaps a two-coach suburban set to be coupled to a set of lavatory vehicles!

As they got older in the LMS period the sets had individual vehicles replaced as necessary, rather than the whole set, thus giving a very varied appearance to trains until either their substitution by DMUs or standard LMS- or BR-built vehicles.

The story of coach development on the LMS follows, at least in the early years, a similar course to

A Fairburn 2-6-4 tank on an evening Blackburn-Manchester service approaches Bolton Trinity Street with an interesting train. The first vehicle is an ex-LNWR motor car van to Diagram 186, followed by an ex-LNER vehicle, then LMS Period II stock. In the sidings behind the train is a sign of things to come, Cravens two-car DMUs, which, along with the Derby Lightweight and Metro-Cammell sets, began to make serious inroads into passenger workings in the early '60s. Surprisingly it seemed to be the middle-distance or cross-country services that first used DMUs. *D. Hampson*

that of locomotive development, being at first based on Midland Railway practices. The influence of the former Midland Railway and the consequent problems it caused, not least in the slow development of locomotive practice, has been well documented elsewhere and is hardly appropriate here. Suffice to say that it took ten years before the familiar steel flush-sided vehicles came into production, and during the life of coach construction on the LMS there were distinctive periods of design. These are commonly described as Periods I, II and III, lasting roughly from 1923 to 1929, 1929 to 1932 and 1933 until the end of the LMS.

This reference to the three periods is in itself interesting as it was, I believe, developed as a convenient way of identifying LMS coach building styles by David Jenkinson and Bob Essery in the studies they undertook into LMS coaches. It has now become the standard means of identification and was even used by BR.

The basic features distinguishing each period reflected the evolution of design and materials used in the construction. Period I coaches were wooden-bodied with matchboard ends and steel underframes, semi-elliptical roofs and twin window arrangements, at compartments and vestibule areas - a Midland Railway characteristic. Fifty-seven feet become the standard coach length, although coaches were built to other underframe lengths. Single window arrangements began to appear in 1928 and the first all-steel vehicles were introduced in 1926, but were of the two-window style and finished in a representation of the fully panelled coaches.

The main characteristic of Period II coaches was the adoption of the Stones or Dewel window ventilators and the single window for corridor stock, also the deepening of windows with the consequent elimination of the waist panel. However, two-window, high-waisted corridor composites continued to be built for some time, and coaches were still wooden-bodied. A batch of 57-foot vestibule coaches and 69-foot dining cars were constructed of steel panelling with pseudo-beading painted on for the fully lined livery of the period. Non-corridor stock of this epoch remained high-waisted and of steel panelling with no beading.

Period III coincides broadly with the arrival of William Stanier as CME of the LMS and the flush-sided coaches introduced shortly after his arrival are for ever associated with his name, though whether he had much to do with coach design is debatable. 'Stanier' coaches were characterised by their flush steel sides, large windows with rounded corners and yet another change in ventilators, this time to sliding ones, initially shallow, but from 1934 much deeper. Roofs now changed in character with steel panelling and ribs crossing from side to side. Torpedo ventilators gave way to shell types. This period of coach development is also noteworthy with the introduction of 60-foot vehicles, primarily Open 1sts, Corridor Composites and Corridor Brake Composites; 57 feet, however, remained the most common length.

This period also saw the removal of lights from above the guard's ducket and the introduction of the simple livery. Many 'Stanier' coaches were built by BR, the most significant change usually being the 'porthole' toilet window and a slight change in profile.

Passenger train formation

Passenger services on the LMS continued for the most part as they had with the pre-Grouping companies, perpetuating the characteristics of those companies, for example the generally higher proportion of 3rd Class accommodation on the Central Division (former Lancashire & Yorkshire) and the use of shorter express trains on the Midland Division.

Passenger workings were, however, not haphazard. The LMS had very detailed marshalling arrangements for passenger trains, which specified the type of vehicles to be used. Generally there were certain patterns, such as marshalling 1st Class accommodation at one end of the train and the provision of a large amount of through workings split from main-line trains. Vehicles for this latter purpose were usually single Brake Composites (Corridor) or a Brake 3rd and Composite where one vehicle wasn't adequate.

While express trains had a large proportion of 3rd Class accommodation in open coaches, lesser workings tended to be formed from inter-district sets, which could either be combined or have strengthening vehicles added. Typically an inter-district set would comprise a Corridor Brake 3rd, Corridor Composite and Corridor Brake 3rd. As with the LNWR formations earlier, many of these could be made up of vehicles from different periods including pre-Grouping types, giving quite a variety in appearance.

If you are considering building a layout set in the North West of England you will probably need to consider the excursion train. These trains employed essentially what was available - remember that prior to the 1970s there was spare stock available to strengthen trains and form additional ones if required to cope either with special workings or to respond to demand - a far cry from today! As the BR Mk I stock increased in numbers in the mid-'50s, pre-Grouping corridor stock was displaced from principal services, often being either stored or in turn displacing other

This pair of pictures are included to show the changing formation of basically the same train. The first is an East Lancashire to Blackpool service in 1937 headed by an ex-L&Y 0-6-0 and with a mixture of early L&Y and LMS standard stock, mostly of Periods I and II. The second shot is of an ex-LMS 'Crab' in 1964 on a similar service. The loco has changed and the coaches are all of LMS origin. *Author's collection*

stock on services lower down the pecking order. However, in the North West, where excursion traffic was still a major consideration, many coaches were stored after withdrawal pending use in such seasonal traffic. They were often patched up and I doubt whether they were cleaned from one year to the next. One location where carriages were thus stored was near Tyldesley, where it was not uncommon to see repairs comprising sheets of metal screwed over rotting wood panels on door bottoms - even tongue and groove planking,

unpainted, filling in rotten panelling. Just imagine, not only a railway with spare carriages, but one with sidings in which to store them!

In considering the position for suburban and local services, the picture outlined for the LNWR period was not much changed. Non-corridor lavatory stock was favoured for longer distances and, while sets were made up and marked, they were usually anything but standard in appearance, being created by type of vehicle rather than style. Indeed, the process of replacing individual vehicles as necessary continued. Consequently, until the 1960s for most services the common modeller's image of trains of similar styles of vehicles was the exception rather than the rule.

Before leaving the prototype coaching scene and moving on to the models, it is worth taking a brief look at what is commonly referred to as the 'push-pull train'. This is common on model railways and also

very convenient. The term 'push-pull' is, however, not the only one used; the LMS referred to these trains as 'motor fitted', and the coaches were branded 'Psh Pll'.

The LMS inherited considerable numbers of such vehicles and built a good many itself, although they were not specifically designed as such and were to all intents and purposes modifications of standard non-corridor stock with very little external changes in appearance save for windows in the driving trailer end and the operating gubbins of additional pipework, etc. These vehicles were built new from 1949, although there were a number of conversions; a batch of the new vehicles arrived at Great Moor Street in 1949-50, and the LNWR-built push-pull coaches disappeared very quickly. The only Period I vehicles converted were a handful of 54-foot coaches, all other motor fitted vehicles being 57 feet.

The LNWR, like other companies, introduced them for reasons of economy, and this type of service had become formally established by 1910. Many of the vehicles used were converted from existing stock, usually older vehicles rather than new building, although the LNWR did build some new open vehicles for this purpose. A bewildering variety of vehicles were converted for use in motor fitted trains, and many lasted into the BR era.

The LNWR also built self-propelled vehicles, the well-known 'railmotor', and while not strictly appropriate for Platt Lane, I am rather fond of them because they are ideal for many modelling situations.

Traffic requirements for the model

Judging by the number of model railway layouts seen with pre-nationalisation-liveried locomotives pulling British Railways Mk I stock, modellers are either tempted to copy what they see in preservation or give little consideration to the composition of the trains on their layouts. I think the least they could do is to have the correct coaches and liveries to match the locomotive, but then I am just articulating one of my pet hates. It is worse when it comes to wagons. How many '9Fs' did you see pulling trains of indiscriminate mixes of vehicles from private owners to modern air-braked stock? I am a member - just - of the Steam Age generation and can remember steam in the Platt Lane period, but I was only a small boy, and in any event, memory is very fickle. It is, however, relatively easy to get a feel for the area by referring to the many excellent books now available, for example the 'British Railways Past & Present' series, which covers railways in the post-war era, area by area.

I think the reason that I have such an aversion to such anomalies is that I am trying, as I have said repeatedly before, to create an image, a 3D moving picture, recreating some of the atmosphere of the railway rather than modelling individual items to museum standards. Accordingly, the composition of trains, their livery and the resultant overall impression and image is more important to me than the correct number of rivets on the underframe.

If you have followed the story so far, we now need to apply this basic philosophy to our passenger trains. To do this we need to look at what services we are providing and how such trains were made up at the time in the area of our model.

As the layout could have been modelled at any period from the 19th century to, I suppose, the present day ('bus shelter' and Class 142?), it is worthwhile looking at the train formations at various peri-

ods. This also gives some illustration of how coaches developed and designs changed.

Essentially, the services we are providing from Platt Lane are to Manchester (Exchange) and a connecting service for Liverpool (via the equivalent of Kenyon Junction). There would also be the possibility of a couple of through services a day to Liverpool and excursion traffic or a through coach or two to North Wales.

As we have seen, in LNWR days around the turn of the century there were a great many six-wheel vehicles in service and it is probable - confirmed by photographic evidence - that these would still be common in services to Manchester and the connecting services.

An interesting but perfectly acceptable formation for the Manchester services would be a mix of two 30-foot six-wheel coaches, including a Brake 3rd, 42-foot radial stock, probably by 1900 mounted on bogies, and/or a representative of the 50-foot bogie stock.

As the LNWR period progressed the six-wheelers would be replaced with other stock, probably 50-foot vehicles, and the 42-foot vehicle may well have been replaced. A 57-foot vehicle may have been introduced. A Brake 3rd Composite and Brake 3rd could well have been the formation, and, prior to that, two six-wheel 3rds, a 42-foot composite and/or a 50-foot Brake 3rd. However, photographs I have seen of these services prior to the First World War didn't always show the neat arrangement of a brake coach at either end, and some consisted of two six-wheelers and one bogie brake coach!

Little would have changed during the LMS period save for the replacement of vehicles as necessary. The choice, however, is not just a simple one of introducing LMS standard designs. The pre-Grouping vehicles inherited by the LMS began to be spread around and a very common formation from the late 1920s would have been a mixture of LNWR and L&Y vehicles. By the 1930s LMS vehicles could be introduced into the 'set' and a common combination out of Great Moor Street was a three-coach set comprising an ex-LNWR cove-roof Brake 3rd (Diagram 333), LMS Period II Composite and ex-L&Y 56-foot Brake 3rd (Diagram 95). This formation was still around well into the 1950s; in the early '50s trains on the Great Moor Street to Exchange services were made up of literally anything that happened to turn up in Ordsall Lane Carriage Sidings, from ancient to post-war corridor stock. By 1960, however, there would have been a much more uniform look about the train with the use of 'Stanier' 57-foot corridor stock. This would have been side-corridor stock, though any strengthening could well have been by open stock.

DMUs would have begun to appear at this time and

Right On the subject of train formation, here on a stormy summer's day in 1960 leaving Bolton for Preston is a Stanier 2-6-4 tank and a mix of ex-LMS Period I, II and III non-corridor stock. *D. Hampson*

Middle right Almost the Platt Lane non-corridor train, an Ivatt Class '2' 2-6-2T with an ex-L&Y, LNWR and LMS three-coach set strengthened with a fourth, LMS, vehicle leaves Bolton Great Moor Street in 1951. Note that the Ivatt is push-pull-fitted but is not hauling an auto-fitted train. *Author's collection*

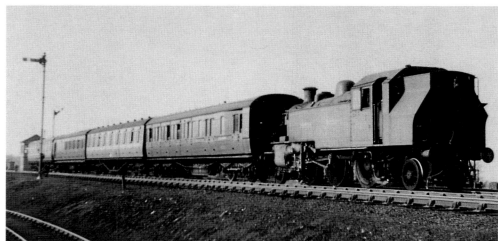

Bottom right Here in model form is a Diagram M56 push-pull train heading into a far from complete Platt Lane station. The vehicles are in early LMS fully lined livery and comprise a Diagram M56 Driving Trailer 3rd and Diagram 87 Third, both of LNWR origins and from Chowbent Castings kits.

would have taken over some but not all of the services. The choice of DMU lies between Derby Lightweight (the later ones with the more conventional end), Metro-Cammell two-car sets or Cravens two-car sets. All worked in the area.

The connecting service, the Kenyon Junction equivalent from Great Moor Street, would initially have been of four- and six-wheel vehicles, and would later have been replaced by motor trains; there was a motor train service between Manchester and Bolton Great Moor Street via Tyldesley, near Leigh (goodness knows why anyone would travel that route between the two destinations, as there were quicker alternatives, as the map of railways in the area on page 8 shows). This service disappeared around 1950-51 and had been provided by LNWR cove-roof vehicles of Diagram M56, Motor Driving Trailer Composites, which had been converted from 50-foot cove-roof stock from Manchester Exchange district sets. These vehicles were commonly paired to Diagram 285 all-3rd vehicles. The last locomotives operating these Great Moor Street services were auto-fitted LMS-designed Ivatt 2-6-2 tanks. One point worth noting is that the LMS converted these vehicles from regulator control via rodding to their standard vacuum control during the 1930s.

I would like to think that, say around 1906, the

LNWR might just have tried out one of its six new steam railmotors on this connecting service, and that would give me the opportunity to run one of my favourite models. However, as the last survivor beyond 1931 was sent to the Moffat branch in Scotland, where it soldiered on until 1948, it is hardly a consideration for Platt Lane. Ah, such is reality!

Even had the Great Moor Street services survived beyond 1954 the two-coach 'push-pull' sets would have disappeared around this time; in fact they disappeared from this service in 1953. The intervening period until the DMU arrived - assuming that the service survived - would therefore have been covered in all probability by a standard LMS two-coach motor-fitted set of Period III; in fact these vehicles took over for the last few months of service.

It is quite likely that the through service to Liverpool would have had an inter-district lavatory set or possibly even an inter-corridor set. This gives the opportunity for some variety within the passenger stock and keeps things within the realms of possibility. During LMS and early BR days there were no differences in the stock on Manchester and Liverpool services; indeed, at least one early morning train to Liverpool used stock that worked up from Exchange the same morning.

Despite all the orderly logic, however, when we consider the provision of the passenger service for Platt Lane we must recognise that the prototype

threw up some, on the face of it, very peculiar offerings, which we as modellers would have been hard pressed to dream up. The first of these was the appearance of GWR coaches in Great Moor Street, which came about not because of any through services to GWR territory but because GWR services came into the LNWR's Manchester Exchange, and, while waiting for a return working to Chester later in the day, were often pressed into use on local services; 1929 Collett stock would appear to be the type most commonly involved.

There was also a period in the 1940s when former North Staffordshire Railway vehicles were seen in the area, and these did turn up in this period on Great Moor Street services from Manchester. In addition the former Midland Railway was surprisingly not exempt from providing the stock for services to Great Moor Street in the shape of 48-foot Bain arc roof suburban district sets, a number of which ran in the Manchester area. Unusually, having emphasised the variety in coach 'sets', these appear to have stayed together, at least from the photographs I have seen, with vehicles of the original sets remaining until being scrapped in the late 1950s. The photographs I have seen of them on Manchester to Great Moor Street services are during and immediately after the Second World War, and while it is easy to imagine wartime operating conditions being responsible for their use, it is more than likely that, like the Great Western coaches, they were around, but being allocated to the Manchester District anyway, formed a pool of coaches available to the operating staff for use as needed. They also have an advantage for space-starved modellers in that they were only 48-foot vehicles and therefore relatively short. The disadvantage of these vehicles is that they were in four-coach sets, so they didn't save much space.

This reference to the length of coaches is worth emphasising. Where possible I have used pre-Grouping vehicles and 57-foot LMS vehicles, which, while correct for the period and location of the model, are also relatively short, so help to create the illusion of space because they don't fill the platforms or look too overpowering as, for example, 64-foot BR Mk I stock would. In suggesting passenger stock for the various periods in which the layout might have been set, you will notice that I have kept

I am rather partial to passenger brake vans and fitted van and parcel trains, something that seemed to be very common in my youth. Modellers often make the mistake of going for modern vehicles such as the LMS Stove R or sticking purely to vehicles with origins in their region. Even pre-nationalisation, if you study photographs carefully, trains contained vehicles from several companies and often rather odd assortments. Modellers find Stove Rs attractive, but their appearance was far less common than other vehicles. However, here is the exception that proves the rule, a very minimalist van train, ideal for Platt Lane - 'Black Five', Stove R and two fitted vans approaching Bolton *circa* 1960. *D. Hampson*

train lengths down to a minimum, not only in terms of vehicle lengths but also the overall train length. This question of length is invariably a problem on models, especially so in O gauge where the sheer bulk of 7 mm scale vehicles can 'take over' a layout visually. In trying to present an overall picture and atmosphere I have tried to minimise the impact of the railway itself. One thing in particular that I have tried to avoid is filling the platforms and sidings with stock, as this seems to exacerbate the overwhelming of the layout by the trains.

Avoidance of the longest vehicles where possible is a positive help in this, for example in the LNWR period using six-wheel, 42-foot and 50-foot vehicles, during the LMS period sticking where possible to shorter pre-Grouping types and 57-foot rather than 60-foot vehicles (there was plenty of such stock around until *circa* 1967/68), and for the BR period avoiding the 64-foot standard stock.

Modelling coaching stock

The main constraint in the choice of coaches may be what is available either ready to run or in kits, unless you are prepared to build from scratch. Thankfully today we are in the fortunate position, at least in 4 and 7 mm scales, that most of our requirements can be met from kits. Usually coach kits are of one of the following types:

Aluminium body shells with pre-formed integral roofs and usually cast metal ends, detail parts and bogies.

Etched brass kits, which may or may not be pre-shaped and which usually incorporate cast detail parts and either etched or cast bogies.

Plastic kits, of which there are some very nice LNWR plastic examples in 4 mm scale (not to mention GWR and others), but only very limited numbers in 7 mm scale.

As there are so few plastic coach kits in 7 mm scale they are not really relevant to our consideration of the stock for Platt Lane. However, having built several 4 mm scale plastic kits over the years I would draw

your attention to the plastic wagons we have constructed - the techniques are exactly the same. I would, however, stress the need to be very careful in removing parts from their sprues as they can be easily broken, particularly the finer details in 4 mm scale. The way to help avoid difficulties here is to use a very sharp scalpel blade and support awkward shapes that are preventing the components from being laid down flat on the cutting block. Be careful, too, when fixing glazing. It is the easiest thing in the world to allow the solvent to run over the 'window', so apply it sparingly and be careful to avoid embedding solvent-etched fingerprints there too!

Kits based on an aluminium coach body have been around for a good many years and basically come in two types, those with integral roofs and pre-formed sides and those with separate roofs and sides. These kits invariably represent flush-sided vehicles and are

The typical contents of a 7 mm scale aluminium body coach kit. It calls for little comment, only to reassure modellers that from this rather uninspiring-looking selection of components, a very acceptable model will result, as we shall see over the next few pictures.

Having clearly swotted up on the prototype we are modelling and any instructions that might be provided, we need to look at the components supplied, see how they are likely to fit, choose whether we want to replace or improve any, whether additional parts are required and ascertain whether we need to make any amendments for the vehicle we want.

In this case we are building a 7½-compartment Open 3rd, which will provide the spare or strengthening coach for our corridor services.

Whilst we are looking at the parts and deciding on our best method of proceeding, we should also be looking to see what preparation is needed before assembly, such as cleaning flash from castings, tidying up punched window openings, etc. Invaluable tools for this are small files, old craft knives - used as scrapers - and fine wet and dry paper.

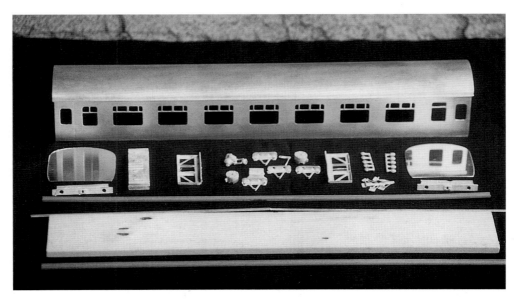

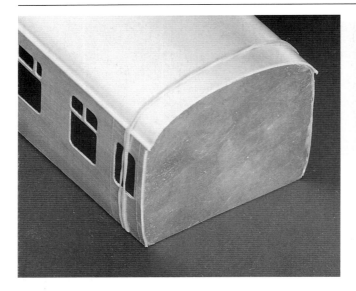

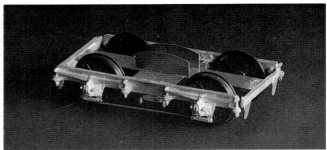

Above The bogies used for this O gauge kit of an LNWR Diagram 333 vehicle (of which more later) are cast white metal and etched brass for the standard LNWR 9-foot wheelbase. As already discussed with regard to wagons, much has been written about compensation and springing for coach bogies and some very ingenious solutions have been offered. However, I have not, so far, found there to be much need - I haven't gone looking for work! In my experience the first priority is to ensure that the bogie is square and accurate in its assembly and that the wheels run freely with minimum side play, thus limiting the risk of them fouling brake or other detail.

The second priority is to ensure that the wheels don't foul the floor. Generally there is some opportunity to place a washer between the bogie rubbing plate and the mounting without raising the buffer height. Providing that you don't overdo it and create another problem of the bogie having too much vertical movement, this should prevent the problem. Some vertical movement is helpful, but it only need be very slight. Experimenting will give you the best solution.

This etched bogie frame already has provision in its design to keep the body at the correct height and allow good movement through two upright fins in the centre.

Above The basic body shell can now be joined to its ends, and any internal partitions. Because these internal partitions are also part of the interior 'detail', mark their location on the outside of the body and of course ensure that they are square. Ends and partitions will need to be fixed with epoxy, but don't overdo it and let the glue spread everywhere - it will cause difficulties later. This business with the partitions generally only applies to the suburban coach; in virtually all other cases the partitions can be built up as part of the interior. Indeed, the only need to put them in as described is because the coach is narrower at the bottom than at the waist, and while you might be able to spring the body over one or two partitions, it would be very difficult to do so over seven! This is really where the advantage of a separate roof is seen. In the case of our Open 3rd it is not a problem.

So far as the ends are concerned, those supplied often have detail such as jumper cables and junction boxes, steps, etc, cast on. I don't think this gives a good enough representation in O gauge and therefore prefer to make my own - a simple job for plain ends, using the casting as a pattern. I will use brass, nickel, tinplate, whatever is to hand, which is of course glued into place.

The shape of the ends is important as it keeps the correct profile, so be careful when cutting them out. For ends with much relief detail such as, say, the Period I matchboard ends, the metal end is inset slightly and a detailed plasticard overlay applied.

Put the body shell on one side for a day or two with rubber bands around it to keep the ends in place and ensure that it is not twisted, otherwise you will have a lot of problems later.

Below The underframe for these coaches is often nothing more sophisticated than a block of wood. Check that it fits neatly and, if it doesn't, sand or cut it until it does. These floors form the bases of the underframe and are generally held in place by being fixed to a ledge on the inside of the ends.

There is the opportunity to provide as much detail as you want on the underframe. I always think it is important to reflect what can be seen in a good clear photograph, but increasingly it is advisable to incorporate all the brake pulls, dynamos, vee hangers, air brake reservoirs, etc. Most of these and cross members for the underframe structures as well as the more easily seen battery and control boxes and material for the truss rods will usually be provided. If it isn't there are plenty of manufacturers supplying these parts separately. In fact, if you want to make a super-detailed model you may want to replace some components with more detailed ones or fabricate further detail yourself.

Cast underframe truss rods are now available and when in place are very effective. This view shows the construction of the structural parts of an underframe from such components.

When you have completed your underframe and are sure that it fits the body shell, give it a good test on your layout or over some test track and a point to ensure that it runs without problems. Better to find out now than after you have painted it.

Here is the interior for the Open 3rd, which is primarily seating. This is readily available in 4 and 7 mm scales from plastic extrusions or wooden mouldings (7 mm scale), while the partitions are plasticard, as are the corridor walls. I cheat a little with this type of kit by making the partitions slightly smaller than they should be to fit inside the body. Similar principles are followed for interiors that fit from the top.

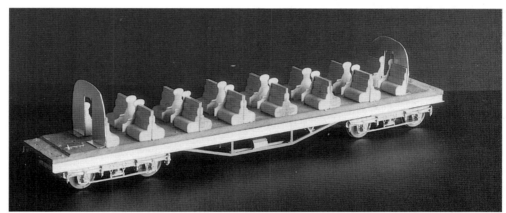

produced by punching out window openings, and scribing door lines into aluminium sheet, which then forms either of the two types of body. Because the window holes are punched, some of the detail such as the framework for the sliding ventilators is perhaps not as fine as it might be with either a moulding or etching. However, these bodies make up into very good representations of the flush-sided stock mentioned earlier.

While it is perfectly possible to solder aluminium with special fluxes and solder, it is not easy, particularly when trying to fix it to, say, a white metal end casting. Consequently ends and other components generally need to be glued in place on the body shell with epoxy resin. I always 'rough up' the areas to be glued to help adhesion.

There is usually a wooden floor in 7 mm scale kits of this type, to which underframe detail is attached in the form of castings and truss rods, etc, for which brass section is provided. One advantage of this type of construction is the ability to remove the underframe from the body to allow interior detail to be made up. I think this is important in both 4 and 7 mm scale coaches; it adds time to the construction but is worth it, not least for the satisfaction of knowing you've done it. I have enclosed some illustrations showing how this can be achieved. With slight variations depending on the design of the kit it is usually possible to add an interior this way or on a false floor from the top.

It is generally necessary to drill out for door handles, grab handles, roof ventilators, etc, and care needs to be taken to ensure that such holes are properly lined up - nothing looks worse than a drunken line of ventilators or door handles! I use a fine indelible felt pen for this marking out. Make the holes appropriate to the components you are going to fit in them. Generally, cast ventilators will require much bigger holes than the hand rails and door handles. It is better at this stage to have the holes undersized - you can always open them up later.

Door handles are available ready made from the trade (or file your own up from brass pins). I prefer to paint over them and scrape the paint off afterwards, rather than risk damaging the paintwork by gluing the handles in place after painting.

The accompanying photographs show the general assembly of these kits and explain further the methods used in their construction.

The next type of coach kit to consider is the etched brass variety. This type of kit probably makes up the majority on the market in 4 and 7 mm scale and comes into its own when earlier panelled coaches are modelled, the etching process making the rendition of full panelling and beading, matchboard sides and ends and other multi-layer external details straightforward. In addition the etching process lends itself to representing clearly the finely intricate shapes and cut-outs such as sliding ventilators.

The answer to the question of which type of kit is better than another lies in the type of vehicle being modelled, where, as suggested above, the method of reproducing the various components will reflect the type of vehicle. Whatever sort you choose you will have to spend time and patience on it; to produce good, reliable models we have to get away from the 'shake the box and it falls into place' notions that the old two-bob Airfix aeroplane kits may have given us. Having said that, there is nothing involved beyond the capabilities of almost anyone, providing that patience, care and a little thought and pre-planning is put into the job. And the rewards - well, they're there as testimony that your efforts were worth it.

As with any model, familiarise yourself with your chosen subject - the kit and above all the instructions - before you begin, for even though the instructions may be sparse, nothing more than a sketch and a couple of sentences in some cases, they should give some idea of what the manufacturer has intended and, studied together with photos and drawings of the real thing, will ensure that when you begin construction you know what you are doing - or at least what the box of bits in front of you should look like when you've finished.

Ensure, too, that you are aware of any detail alterations or modifications during a vehicle's life that may affect the external appearance or choice of parts, for example the conversion to electric lighting or the change from torpedo to shell roof ventilators.

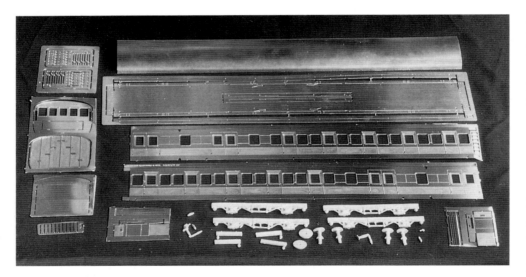

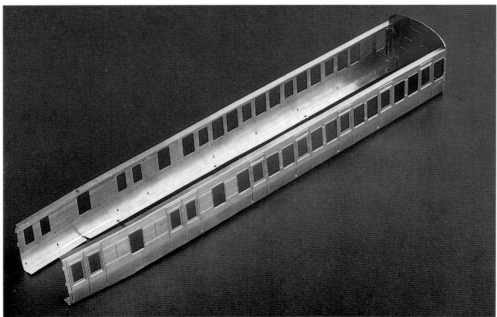

Left Etched brass coach kits provide a different set of challenges and require a different approach from the aluminium body shell based kits previously considered, not least because they require the builder to solder parts together. This is a relatively easy, straightforward basic technique that all modellers need to master.

This kit, shown in component form, is the Chowbent Castings Lancashire & Yorkshire Diagram 94 56-foot non-corridor Brake 3rd, forming part of our non-corridor set. The contents are typical of etched coach kits. The first assembly work is usually the bogies, which present nothing too complicated. The plate glass base is once again essential to ensure a square and accurate assembly.

Left and top right In common with many etched coaches, this one requires folds along its length. Folding brass with bending bars has been mentioned elsewhere, but suffice it to emphasise here the need for care to avoid distorting the side. Most coaches have a curve or 'tumblehome' to their sides, which should reflect the profile of the ends. Here you don't want sharp bends but a gentle curve. Place the side inside up on a surface with some give in it and roll a tube over it, rather like rolling pastry, until you have the shape;

ensure that the tube is longer than the side. I keep a few odd lengths of plastic and copper piping left over from plumbing jobs for this purpose.

Here you can see the sides of the Diagram 94 when formed and soldered to the ends and the underframe, and the solid one-piece floor, which has had the headstocks and solebars bent down and the step-board soldered in place via the slot and tab location.

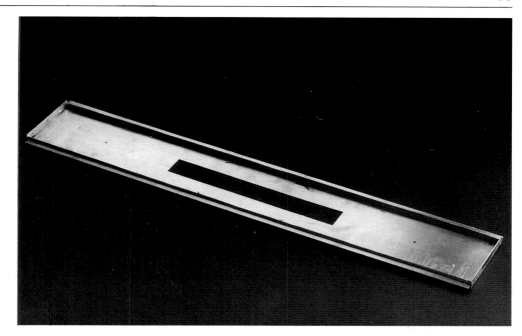

Middle right A close-up shot of the Diagram 94 floor pan showing the folded-down head-stocks and solebars and the stepboard soldered in place located by the slots and tabs.

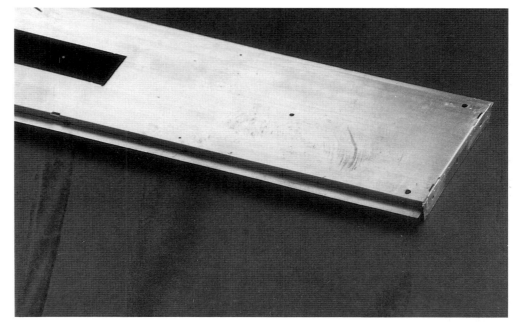

Bottom left and right If you have formed the tumblehome correctly it should be a simple job to solder the coach ends in place from the inside. I prefer to add the detail to the sides and ends after the basic box of the body has been formed, assuming that you can position the parts and get at them after the body shell is assembled but it is a matter of choice. This view of the basic shell under construction for the Diagram 94 vehicle shows the end soldered in place. The slots in the ends are to allow end steps to be passed through and soldered on the inside for strength and neatness.

Door hinges and droplights are usually also fixed from the inside and, depending on the overall design of the coach, you may find it easier to fix these before assembling the sides and ends. These are on the Diagram 333 vehicle.

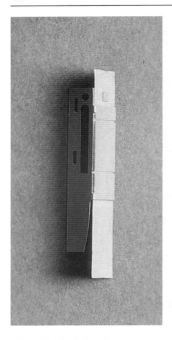

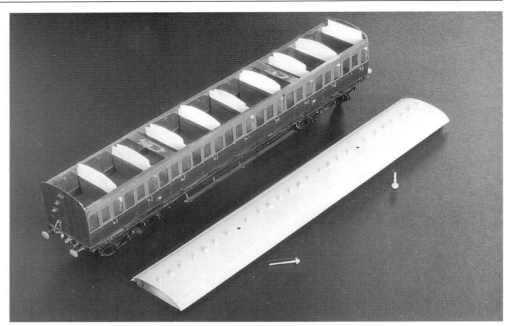

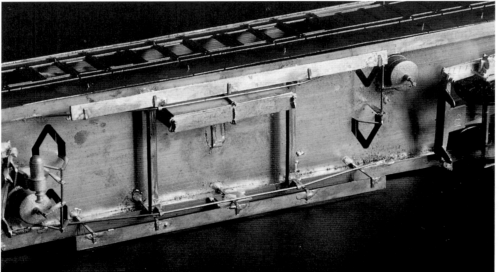

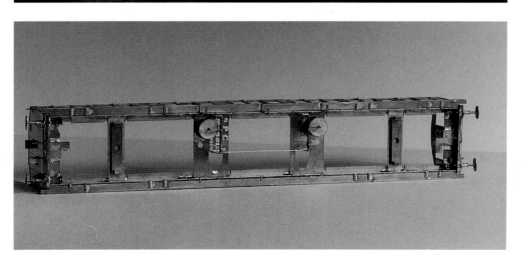

Top left The Diagram 94 vehicles had inset guard's areas to afford a better view along the train. This allowed maximum carriage width and therefore maximum passenger accommodation! In the model, as seen earlier, the body sides are bent inwards and a ducket fixed between them and the coach end. Here is the fabrication showing the locating slots.

Top right The coach also has a pre-formed brass roof, and here is one fixing option. Lamp tops are soldered to bolts that screw into nuts soldered across stretchers at cantrail level. Another option is nuts soldered on the underside of the roof and bolts passed through similar cross stretchers and accessed with a screwdriver through holes cut in the floor.

Middle and bottom There are many variations on floors and underframes in etched kits ranging from the brass floor panel, from which detail such as vee hangers for brakes are bent downwards, to those that are little more than a skeleton and require either a plastic or wooden floor to be added, as in this PC Models kit of a Clayton 48-foot carriage. Some employ a wooden floor.

This is a finished Diagram 94 Brake 3rd in fully lined LMS livery as it may have appeared in the 1940s. Note the roof detail added from castings and wire. This is a key Platt Lane vehicle, but in BR livery.

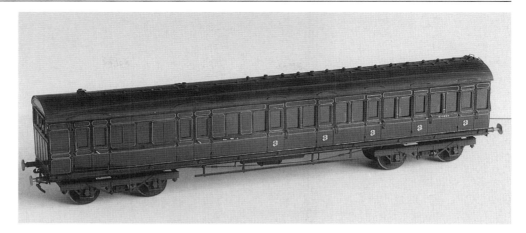

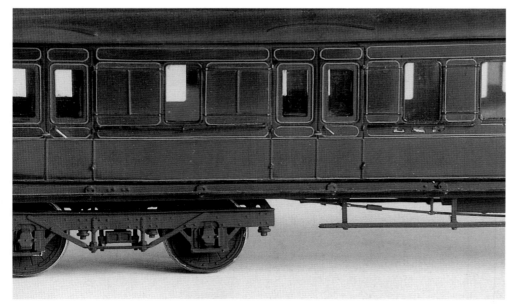

Middle left and left The completed Diagram 94 in LMS livery, detailed and weathered. Note the dirt accumulated around the door hinges, etc; this can be represented with thin washes of paint that sticks in the door and other openings and around panelling as in the end view. It can also be dry brushed on to the underframes.

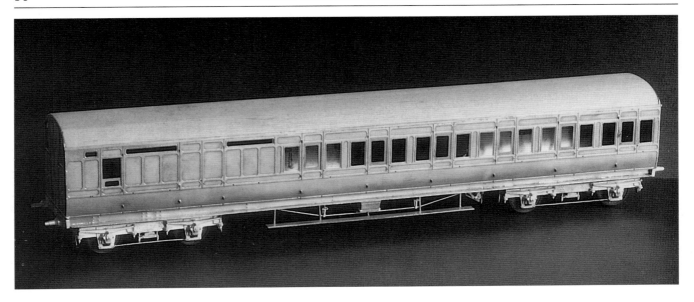

An ex-LNWR Diagram 333 Brake 3rd nearing completion from a Chowbent kit; this is again a key vehicle for Platt Lane. Apart from a different roof, wooden as opposed to brass, the basic construction is similar to that of the Diagram 94. The roof will be covered with fine tissue paper before painting to give a more realistic texture and hide the wood-grain.

Painting and lining coaching stock

Perhaps the biggest single difficulty and worry, after soldering, is painting the finished model, because here, for the first time in coaches, we encounter the essential need for a good finish. A poor paint job can ruin an otherwise excellent model, while a good paint job can improve an ordinary model out of all expectation.

Don't worry, however - it's not that hard to get a good paint finish, as we will see. Painting and lining is a straightforward operation, and while lining out panelling on older vehicles with fully lined liveries is quite tricky, with patience and a little practice a satisfying result can be achieved.

The body should be prepared to provide a smooth, clean surface on which to apply the paint. Once any imperfections have been filled, smoothed and cleaned, the model can be primed. With plastic sides I find cleaning will principally require the removal of dust and plastic filings, etc, which congregate, hidden away, only to emerge to show through the paint; a photographer's lens-cleaning brush with its squeezy blower is useful for this work. With metal sides it is a question of removing residues of glue, flux and grease, and once again cigarette lighter fuel *carefully* applied with a cotton pad is excellent for this.

Priming is the next consideration, and the same comments as those made regarding goods stock apply here (see page 38).

It is worth noting, however, that colour applied to locomotives and coaches causes as much controversy as any other aspect of the hobby. Irrespective of manufacturing or technical reasons for colour changes, colour is a very personal thing, and each of us may well perceive a colour in a particular, yet slightly different, way - and that takes no account of colour blindness. My view is that the matched colour ranges such as Rail Match are quite accurate enough, although there is usually a car aerosol paint that is a pretty good match for a railway colour; for example, I use Austin-Rover Damask Red for LMS/BR Maroon. I mask the window openings from the inside - the exterior colour should not come through to the interior. If you paint the interior walls and partitions to represent a lighter, more modern finish or a darker wood, again use an aerosol spray of the appropriate colour, but paint the inside before the outside as it is less of a problem if the masking tape used on the windows is applied on the inside and causes some minor damage to the paint than if the paint was 'lifted' by the tape on the outside.

I think spraying is essential to get a nice, even gloss finish on coaching stock. The whole body sides are sprayed using several light coats to build up the colour rather than one heavy coat. When they are fully dry and the paint has had a little time to harden, the body sides can be masked with tape and the roof ends painted. It will be necessary on some vehicles to paint the droplights a different colour from the main body sides, and this must be done with a fine brush. Where the livery requires a two-tone body side, the body can be sprayed in the lighter colour, then when this has dried it can be masked with tape and the darker colour applied.

Many of the vehicles used on Platt Lane had a long life and could be finished in a variety of liveries to suit the period of your layout, but watch for detail difference such as the removal of gas lighting, changes in classification, etc. These pictures show a selection of vehicles in various liveries, but even though liveries may have officially changed at a given date, vehicles generally continued to carry their existing livery until repainting was due. These vehicles from Chowbent Castings kits are in Lancashire & Yorkshire, early LMS and mid-1930s LMS liveries.

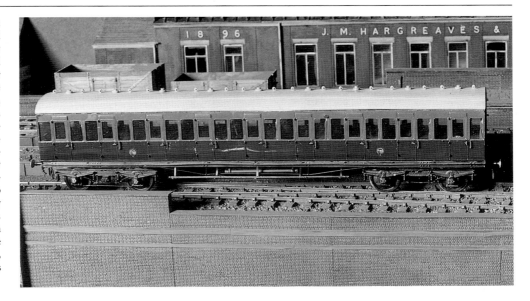

The varnished teak livery of the LNER and some other pre-Grouping companies is difficult to represent. There have been many methods detailed in the model railway press on achieving this finish with excellent results; the simplest method I have found, which is quite effective but, I accept, not necessarily the best possible, is to spray the body sides cream and to apply with a brush a quite fluid wash of a suitable brown, tan or similar shade. The idea is to let the cream base just show in fine streaks through the brown; it may be necessary to apply more than one coat of brown.

Lining out coaches is not as difficult as it seems at first glance, particularly with simple liveries requiring only straight lines. There are some lining transfers available for certain liveries and these will either be of the waterslide or press-fix

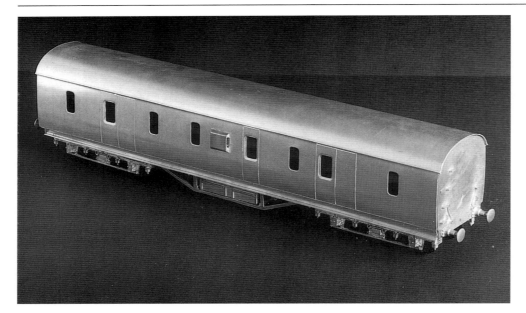

Unfortunately the materials that suit our model-making are not always the best for painting; neither aluminium nor brass are particularly good at holding paint. A good primer is therefore essential and there are a number of self-etch primers on the market, specially formulated for model-making.

For these aluminium shells my preference is to give them a quick rub over with fine wet and dry paper to provide a key for the primer. If you have white metal ends these will need to be burnished until surface marks are removed. I spray the vehicle in primer sold in aerosol cans for car repairs, and find that this gives a good result and dries very quickly. Both the inside and outside of the vehicle are sprayed, and I save myself a further job if the vehicle has a wood panelled interior by spraying with red primer. Primer will enable you to see if any further preparation is necessary to the model before the top coat is applied.

The secret of a good finish is preparation and patience, giving plenty of time for paint to harden before you start applying masking tape or transfers. Here are two views of a 50-foot Full Brake, the first showing the preparation before painting, including added detail and a burnished cast end, and the second showing the same vehicle with the main colours applied.

type. The former, despite any suggestion that it is not necessary, should be trimmed to the exact line, then applied as per the instructions. These transfers can be quite versatile and, with care and the aid of a sharp scalpel, plus a bit of ingenuity, can give a fair representation of the fully panelled livery as applied to flush-sided stock by the LMS at one period.

Long straight lines need some care and the use of a straight edge to check that the transfer is actually straight. If you don't check and adjust at this stage, you're sure to discover that the line is crooked when a coat of varnish has been applied and nothing can be done! Adjustments can be made by moistening the transfer, re-positioning it correctly and smoothing it

down again. It is important to ensure that the transfer is flat down to the surface, and there are some preparations available to ensure that transfers 'lie down' over, for example, rivet detail.

The press-fix type transfers are also quite versatile and can be adapted as described above. Care is also needed to ensure that the lines are straight, and the straight edge is essential. Unlike waterslide transfers, however, they cannot be adjusted when rubbed down fully, so care is needed to ensure that the transfer is straight before it is pressed home and the backing paper removed. This type of lining is very fine and can often be used to good effect on moulded panelling without overhanging the raised mouldings. These lin-

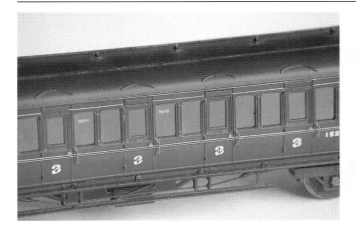

Transfers and painting can add character to your coach, as with the 'Smoking' signs on these compartment windows. Note also the droplight left open on the carriage door in the second picture, and the brass wire handles scraped clean of paint with a sharp craft knife.

ing transfers are generally available only for 4 mm scale, but I find them equally effective in 7 mm scale, particularly the coarser waterslide type.

Lettering is available for all pre-nationalisation and some pre-Grouping companies and BR through to the present day, and vast ranges of transfers and matched paints are also available for North American railways.

When the lining and lettering is complete a coat of varnish (from an aerosol) in gloss or semi-gloss, to taste, should be applied. Coaches, like wagons, need to be weathered to keep up the illusion and help the overall picture, but often this need only be a wash that will leave a residue in door joints and the corners of beading, panelling, etc.

Finally, before leaving coaches, a word about my favoured method of lining, using a pen and paint. This is not as difficult as it seems or as some people would have you believe. Determination and practice will produce a satisfactory result, particularly on simple straight lines. The bowpen, illustrated in the diagram, is filled with paint - a cocktail stick or similar is helpful for this. The paint must be well-stirred new paint and not too thick or too thin - a milky consistency. The width of the line the pen draws is governed by the screw, which adjusts the

pressure on the arch or bow element - tighter for finer lines. Wipe any excess paint from the blades before use, then keep the pen upright and draw a practice line on scrap material; the thickness of the line can then be adjusted and the line drawn properly with the pen against a ruler. The model should be supported to prevent it moving and the ruler should not be rested on the model but on supports. A simple jig for this is shown in the diagram.

Curves can be drawn by this method using a template or French curves. The trick is to keep the pen upright and draw in a steady movement, not dwelling long enough to allow paint to blob or moving too quickly to prevent an even flow. Like most things, practice improves the result. Remember to keep the pen clean and wash the blades in thinners between refills to keep the pen flowing freely.

I paint all my coaches with car touch-up paint, which is cellulose, then line them with Humbrol enamels, which, if I make a mistake, can be wiped away without damaging the cellulose base colour. Whatever base paint you use, allow it to harden for several days before lining by the bowpen method.

Using a bowpen, and a simple support to assist in lining jobs.

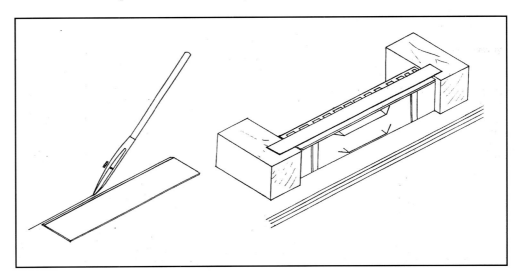

5.
LOCOMOTIVES

The same process that was used for the goods and passenger stock is used to determine the locomotives we need for our layout. Essentially we are looking at the services that we are going to operate, and the appropriate motive power for those services at the period and in the location of our model. There is, however, a new element to consider, and that is the locomotive allocations at the sheds that would have provided this motive power.

It is not difficult to find appropriate prototype shed allocations, but while these can be a guide, sometimes indeed a prescriptive list, shed allocations are more often only a guide as they do not take into account more complex diagramming of available locomotives from the most unlikely sources - locomotives visiting the area, short-term transfers and changes in allocation - or the moving around of locomotives between sheds in a regional grouping to suit short-term expediency.

In an earlier chapter I referred to the services that were being provided from Platt Lane and the sheds that were likely to provide those services. These sheds were primarily, at least so far as the mid-'50s just before closure is concerned, Patricroft, Manchester, Springs Branch (Wigan) and Sutton Oak (St Helens), with Plodder Lane (Bolton), which closed in 1954. British Railways reorganised its sheds in the late 1950s; then Patricroft, for example, no longer came under Springs Branch but now under 26A, Newton Heath - an LNWR shed under an L&Y shed! Springs Branch became 8F, as did Sutton Oak, which became 8G, both then under Edge Hill, Liverpool.

Locomotive choice

Looking at the locomotives that operated the prototype services, it is easy to be quite definite up until Platt Lane's inspiration, Great Moor Street, closed in 1954, but for the period of the model, 1959, we have to deduce from practice in the area at that time, and to do this the best aid is photographs. If we can get photographs clear enough to show shed plates, we can refer back to shed allocations that will reveal a bit more of the story.

If we look at the LNWR period, a large proportion of the Plodder Lane allocation was the celebrated Webb 'Coal Tank'. Other common locomotives were the Webb 5 ft 6 in (driving wheel diameter) 2-4-2 tank, 'Watford' 0-6-2 tanks from the bigger sheds such as Patricroft, and, as we noted earlier, 4-4-0 'Precursors' on any North Wales excursions; our choice of locomotives for passenger services during this period would be from the tank locomotives. I personally would avoid the 'Precursors', beautiful machines though they were, as being perhaps, for want of a better phrase, a little too *exceptional* and therefore detracting from rather than adding to the atmosphere. This question of atmosphere affects not only the selection of the locos and stock but also, as we shall see later, their finish.

The LNWR and L&YR amalgamated in 1922, but at least until well into the LMS period little would have changed so far as the locomotives were concerned. However, the LMS 4-4-0 tender locos of Class '2P' were allocated in the late 1920s to Patricroft and, though decidedly unpopular with LNWR men being basically a Midland loco, they were used and appeared, I have been informed, at Great Moor Street - so why not Platt Lane?

The 1930s also saw perhaps the most sweeping changes on the LMS with the introduction of the Stanier 'Standard' designs, but these would at this pre-Second World War period have had little direct effect on the services we are providing from Platt Lane. Indirectly, however, they did have one effect through displacing other, older locomotives that, when not withdrawn, would be released for lesser duties, and it is possible that this 'shake-down' would have resulted in locomotives moving around sheds and duties.

In the early years of the LMS the aforementioned '2Ps' were not the only newly built locomotives; indeed, the LMS put out new designs under Fowler, most notable for our purposes being the two types of tank locomotives, the 2-6-2 and larger 2-6-4 designs. Both certainly operated in the area and, by the outbreak of war in 1939, the Fowler 2-6-2 types were quite common in Great Moor Street, No 58 being a regular.

The other interesting development during the pre-war LMS period was the increasing use of other LMS constituent companies' locos, with ex-L&Y 2-4-2 tank locomotives, particularly the Belpaire boiler type, becoming quite common on passenger duties.

I have suggested in the accompanying table appropriate locomotives for different periods. You might accuse me of being a bit conservative in my choice, but I have tried to select locomotives that actually provided the services needed for Platt Lane. I have also, as mentioned earlier regarding the 'Precursor', avoided the more glamorous types because of the atmosphere and the need to maintain this overall impression. Larger locomotives also take up more space, and in small layouts where space is at a premium avoidance of filling the layout visually is important. Therefore the smaller locomotives chosen, while representative for our needs, are also better in terms of overall visual appearance.

LNWR period

Passenger services
2 Webb 0-6-2T 'Coal Tanks'
1 Webb 5 ft 6 in 2-4-2T or 1 Webb 0-6-2T
   'Watford' tank
Freight services
1 Webb '17 inch' goods 0-6-0 tender loco
1 Webb 'Cauliflower' 0-6-0 tender loco
Shunting/station pilot
1 Ramsbottom 'Special' 0-6-0 tender loco
Total 6 locos

I have suggested two 'Coal Tanks' because they were synonymous with local passenger services in the area well into the LMS period, and while two of the same type might be regarded as boring by some, it is so typical as being difficult to avoid. You could have a 'Coal Tank' and one each of the others, but this would, I think, stretch the *atmosphere* a bit. In any event you are not obliged to have both 'Coal Tanks' in the station at once!

Early LMS period (up to about 1929)

As above except perhaps a '4F' rather than the '17 inch' goods. Livery would now be LMS, of course, and despite the adoption of different styles at given dates, the variety of liveries on show would be quite considerable - a matter we will touch on when we look at painting the models.

LMS middle period (about 1935)

Passenger services
2 0-6-2T 'Coal Tanks' or 1 with a Webb 5 ft 6 in
   2-4-2T
1 Class '2P' 4-4-0 tender loco or Fowler 2-6-2T
Freight services
1 LMS '4F' 0-6-0 tender loco
1 ex-L&Y Aspinall '3F' 0-6-0 tender loco
Shunting/station pilot
1 Aspinall 0-6-0ST or LMS 'Jinty' 0-6-0T

The same comments apply regarding liveries. In so far as the passenger services are concerned the 'motor' services would require at all periods at least one of the passenger tanks to be 'push-pull' fitted. I would suggest the 5 ft 6 in tank for the first period, the 'Coal Tank' for the second and the Fowler for the 1935 period. The Crook Street shunter was always a 'Jinty' post-war.

The Platt Lane era (1959)

This is where we get into real speculation, drawing on the appropriate shed allocations in the area and the types used on similar services to those we are running.

Passenger services
1 Fairburn 2-6-4T (No 42119 of Springs Branch,
   8F)
1 Ivatt 2-6-2T (No 41287 of Patricroft, 26F)
1 Fowler 2-6-2T (No 40058 of Patricroft)
Freight services
1 Fowler '4F' 0-6-0 tender loco (No 44317 of
   Sutton Oak, 8G)
1 Aspinall '3F' 0-6-0 tender loco
Shunting/station pilot
1 Aspinall 0-6-0ST (No 51441 of Sutton Oak)

One interesting train of the early 1950s was the 5.25pm from Exchange, which was always either a Patricroft 'Black Five' or 'Jubilee', or later often a BR Standard 4-6-0.

BR Standard '2' 2-6-2 tanks were common in the Bolton area, some even appearing at Plodder Lane before its 1954 closure. Here a Horwich-Bolton service is hauled by one such loco. The leading vehicle is interesting, being an LMS-built six-wheel milk van. *D. Hampson*

The freight side would also have provided for a variety of locomotives. In the LNWR period 'Cauliflower', 'DX' and '17-inch' types of 0-6-0 goods locomotive would be typical, but the various Webb eight-coupled goods locomotives from Patricroft and Springs Branch were also common. Shunting and local trip workings in the early LNWR period would be provided by the Ramsbottom 0-6-0 saddle tanks.

The LMS period saw both the Midland '4Fs' and Aspinall 0-6-0s in common use on freight services, and the 'G1/G2' 'Super D' 0-8-0s were usual motive power on mineral and heavier services.

The post-war period is interesting not least because Plodder Lane shed was probably unique in having its allocation of Webb 0-6-2 tank locomotives replaced in one fell swoop by new Ivatt Class '2' 2-6-2 tanks locomotives, and later these were joined by their BR Standard Class '2' versions, which by 1954 had replaced them. Then came the introduction of the Stanier '8Fs' working the heavier services with the 'Super Ds' and the 'WD' 'Austerity' 2-8-0s. Shunting and trip working during the LMS period would see L&Y 0-6-0 saddle tanks, which lasted until the 1960s, and LMS Fowler 'Jinties'.

There is also the possibility to introduce a smaller mixed traffic tender loco at this period, perhaps a 2-6-0 such as a 'Crab', Stanier 'Mogul' or LMS or BR Standard Class '2'. I would choose the latter as being the most appropriate as an additional loco or an alternative to one of the 2-6-2 tank locos. They were quite common in the area in which our model is set and are versatile locos, being seen on services ranging from semi-fast passenger to pick-up freight and even pilot duties.

Modelling locomotives

Now down to business. In selecting the appropriate locos for Platt Lane I have also tried to keep one eye on trying to ensure as much variety as possible in the designs of the kits. This will enable us to cover as many as possible of the common methods and problems that you are likely to encounter. Although we are talking about O gauge, the basic principles apply to many of the kits available in 4 mm scale, so the methods will hopefully have a wide application.

The one exception is the white metal locomotive kit. Full white metal kits are not that common in 7 mm scale except for the Springside GWR types, and these are of such quality as to cause few problems. There is some white metal in the Fairburn kit, and with the earlier discussion on building white metal wagons, I think most aspects will have been covered. I have included one kit that features cast polyester resin body components for one major part; this is a comparatively recent material to appear in kits and one that is becoming more common.

You might balk at the thought of building locomotives from kits, but unless you have a deep wallet and can have them built for you, or you can purchase them ready to run or scratch-built, it is the only way to provide the locomotives you will need, whatever your chosen prototype.

I have deliberately avoided any comment on the subject of quality or ease of assembly. There is a very good reason for this. In my experience building kits is a very personal matter. Notwithstanding major problems of measurements, shape, etc, which do occur from time to time in kits, there are very few that I have encountered - and I've built a good few - that won't give you a decent representation of your chosen prototype. You have I think to consider the amount of effort required to achieve the desired result and bear in mind the overall cost of each particular kit and components. I have been driven to the point of wanting to commit serious physical damage to the 'designers' of kits with which other modellers have had few if any problems. Never has that phrase about 'one man's meat. . . ' been more apt!

Unfortunately the cost of a kit does not always reflect its quality or ease of assembly. You really do have to decide for yourself and take the plunge. If you have only limited experience and, like most of us, would be very concerned at 'wasting' money on a kit that you can't get along with, the best course of action is to visit some exhibitions and talk to the operators of layouts who might have a loco in which you are interested, and ask them how they got on with the model. One word of warning, though: don't jump in and immediately assume that it is a kit. There is nothing more galling than asking about a kit-built loco that is in fact a scratch-built labour of love. Also visit the manufacturers at exhibitions and examine the kits, look for unpainted models and see how well the parts fit (or don't); the absence of filler in a good square model is a good sign, easily shown on unpainted models. Above all, remember that building kits takes time and patience. There is very little that can't be overcome with these ingredients and a dash of ingenuity.

Before moving on, I will issue a word of caution about the sources of information and, above all, the use of drawings and preserved examples. The best source of reference is a good photograph, preferably of the individual loco you are modelling at the time that you are modelling it - very rare! Otherwise photos of the same class at the period, or the same loco at another. But beware of detailed differences, improvements and adaptations, particularly on long-serving or large classes of locomotives. Standard, or so-called standard, classes were often notorious for detail differences, for example the Brighton 'Terriers' and LMS 'Jubilees' to name but two. Interchange of components between earlier and later batches, differences in detail between batches and, particularly in the later BR period, the fitting of any suitable part that was to hand, all help to cause confusion and trap the unwary. Therefore a good familiarisation with the class and the loco you are modelling is needed before we rush out and but the bits and pieces. I have noted some of the differences in the class of the locos we are building for Platt Lane as we go along.

Photographs are therefore, I believe, essential, and drawings are also very helpful but, for kit-building, not essential. Drawings can be misleading, some not being accurate, many only covering a loco as built or at one period. They are sometimes dimensionally inaccurate, so it is worthwhile checking the dimensions with the drawing. I know personally of one builder who complained that a boiler in a kit was 4 mm too short, and another with the same kit who said it was a similar amount over-length! Who'd be a kit manufacturer?

The third and final caution - I'm sounding like a referee - concerns copying preserved examples. Suffice to say here that it is not unusual to find that preserved locomotives have been modified for expediency, perhaps only in a minor way but nevertheless one that can affect the appearance of a model, perhaps a pipe run, or new arrangement such as the fitting of a Giesl injector as in the case of *City of Wells*. Invariably locomotives are preserved as withdrawn, and may be significantly different than at earlier periods in their history. The question of preserved locomotive liveries is yet another matter more properly referred to when we discuss painting and lining later.

The prospect of modelling locomotives, and the assembly of locomotive kits, is for many a daunting one. I hope in the next few pages to show that it needn't be. While you will not find locomotive kits that can be assembled with the ease of the old Airfix plastic kits, you will find that with patience, care and a little common sense you can get a satisfying result.

Many of the steps involved are common across a wide range of locomotives, so to avoid being repetitive I have started by showing in almost step by step detail the first locomotive, the L&Y saddle tank, and followed this by showing in more selective detail the construction of the other locomotives used on Platt Lane; where there is something new or different from the basic practices shown with the saddle tank - for example, milled and etched valve gear, etched chassis, side tanks, tenders, etc - I have concentrated on that.

In the 'Modelling techniques' chapter we have already discussed basic modelling techniques such as soldering, gluing, cutting and shaping materials, cleaning up, etc. I hope this will avoid too much repetition in this chapter, but I would stress that they are largely just my way of doing things and that often there are other approaches. As with most things you develop your own techniques as you gain experience, and what works for you or what you find to be an easier approach may not be so for others.

Lancashire & Yorkshire 0-6-0 saddle tank No 51441

The first locomotive to consider is the smallest and simplest, and the one that features the newer material of resin cast parts. I've chosen to model No 51441 of Sutton Oak (8G) shed.

These locos originated from Barton Wright tender locos and were converted to saddle tanks between 1891 and 1899; there were ultimately 230 such conversions. As was common throughout British locomotive history, there were several different contractors employed on this work, including the railway's own Miles Platting Works, and, not surprisingly, there were detail differences, some resulting from changes in specification as the rebuilding programme progressed. For example, different lengths of saddle tank were required to fit the variety of boilers on the engines being converted, and there were three distinct arrangements of plating making up the saddle tank, noticeable in the varying position and patterns of the rivets. Ultimately only one type of boiler would be adopted for these locomotives, which necessitated modifications to some of the saddle tanks.

One other effect of the early variety in boilers was the need to provide an oval hole in the tank to allow for the variation in the position of the safety valves, which, of course, needed to protrude through the tank. Similarly, Kitson and Sharp Stewart rebuilds had, at least when newly rebuilt, balance weights, while others did not.

Top left The following series of photographs of Aspinall saddle tanks is included to demonstrate the variations of even such a humble class of goods engines, and is typical of the sort of information I would require before beginning a model. Thankfully there are now a great many books that can provide that source.

The first photograph shows L&Y No 236 built (or rebuilt?) by the L&YR at Miles Platting. It has no balance weights and is shown in original condition in 1922. It looks remarkably clean for a shunting loco even at that period. *Barry Lane collection*

Middle left This is a Kitson-built locomotive that has had replacement splashers fitted; many originals had slotted splashers plated over from the inside. The balance weights fitted to the centre drivers to balance the motion can just be seen and were only on the Kitson and Sharp Stewart examples. The smokebox wrapper has clearly visible rivets and, along with the smokebox door, is a later replacement, probably dating from the late L&Y era. The locomotive has Hoy buffers. No 11353 lasted until 1957 and is pictured here in 1938 at Bletchley, testament to the widespread allocation of many L&Y locomotives throughout the LMS system after the Grouping. *Barry Lane collection*

Bottom left Not only shunting locos, the Aspinall saddle tanks were commonly seen on trip and local freight services; indeed, 58 members of the class also had the automatic vacuum brake, which enabled them to be used on passenger-rated and fitted stock. Despite this, I have seen little evidence of them being fitted with anything other than three-link couplings, although there were some with screw types. This view is of LMS No 11479 at Luddendenfoot in 1946; being an unusual rear view it shows plenty of detail for the modeller including the tools laid across the buffer shanks and vacuum pipe. The goods vehicles are an interesting array, the second being an LMS standard ventilated van. The fourth vehicle, a cattle van, is obviously empty, for as already mentioned loaded livestock vehicles had to be positioned behind the locomotive! *Barry Lane collection*

Top right On to BR days, and here is No 51486 being watered. (It hasn't sprouted a sand dome - the dome-like object between the fireman and the cab front is the top of the water column behind the loco.) This unusual broadside is very useful for modellers showing not only typical detail at the time being modelled but also condition. Note that not all this class were vacuum fitted, so be careful which you choose to model if you want that service option to shunt your passenger-rated vehicles. *D. Hampson*

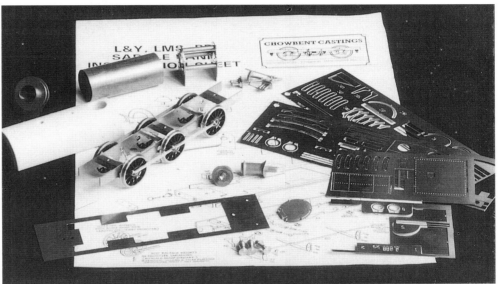

Middle right The main components of the Aspinall saddle tank as supplied in the Chowbent Castings kit, shown with the basic chassis assembled. It requires wheels, motor, gears, transfers, paint and number plates to complete, which is typical of locomotive kits in 4 and 7 mm scales.

Bottom right The first place to start any loco kit is the chassis, and here are views of

the Chowbent Castings saddle tank chassis from above and below. In this case the chassis is of milled brass profile sides screwed together on machined brass spacers.

Assembly should be on a flat surface (I prefer a piece of plate glass), and the frames should be screwed tight to the spacers.

Check that the assembly is square by placing it top down on the plate glass, ensuring that it does not rock. When we have achieved this, we can move on to the bearings and wheel assemblies. Note that the holes in the spacers need to be vertical as the screws fixing the body in place pass through them.

The wheel bearings are pressed into place with the shoulders to the outside. It is often necessary to open out slightly the holes in the sides with a file to enable the bearings to be a good push fit. On this particular chassis the bearings were a tight fit and needed no fixing in place, but I usually find it necessary to solder the bearing in place carefully from the inside, ensuring that no solder gets on to the inside of the bearing.

Next assemble the wheels on to the axles. Nowadays virtually all O gauge wheels have square-ended, shouldered axles that keep the wheels to the right gauge and accurately 'quarter' them.

'Quartering' means that the cranks on opposite sides of the loco are at 90 degrees to each other, thus enabling the stroke of the piston to complete a revolution of the wheels via the coupling rods.

These wheels are Slaters and comprise glass-filled nylon spokes, steel turned rims and enclosed brass locating holes. Note that it may be necessary to clean the edges of the square ended axles to ensure a good fit without forcing and risking damage. Exercise extreme caution here as we do not wish to damage the ends and make the axle a sloppy fit on the wheel. It is usually necessary to run a round file inside the bearings to ensure that the wheels rotate freely - again, don't overdo it.

Fit the crank pins to the wheels, assemble them with the coupling rods and, when they run freely, remove the wheels from the chassis. The solder up the frame spacers from the inside.

The plunger pick-ups are shown in place. Fix the housings for the pick-ups after soldering parts such as the ashpan and guard irons in place to prevent damage to them from the heat of the soldering of these other bits and pieces.

The brakes are hung on pivots that are nothing more than brass rod slid through insulating bearings that fix into pre-drilled holes; I measure a length of rod the exact length of the distance over the wheel rims when assembled on the axles. I assemble the shoes on to the hangers by sweating them in place after tinning, and solder the hangers to the transverse bars running between the hangers at the bottom. These are nothing more than pieces of brass rod, cut as the pivots mentioned above. Sometimes etched parts are provided for this, and if you use them follow the same general principles as for the rods described here. I tend to use the rod in any event.

The hangers are generally quite fine and the holes etched in them usually smaller than the 1 mm diameter of the rod. Overcome this and help secure the strength of the assembly by turning the ends down with a shoulder so that the ends of the rods and pivot fit the etched holes in the hangers. You don't need a lathe - place the rod in the chuck of a 12-volt electric mini drill and hold a needle file to the end.

The shoes and hanger assemblies are of course handed and should be placed hanger-side-down on the glass surface and the rod fixed in the bottom holes between them. A touch of flux, a touch of iron and a sliver of solder and the three components should be fixed together.

The top rod forming the pivot of the brake hangers is put through the chassis and each of the assemblies we have made offered up from below. The holes at the top of the hangers are clipped on the rod and soldered in place - again minimum solder, flux and a hot, clean iron.

You will have noticed that this assembly is free to move on the top pivot. This is to our advantage as it helps to get the wheels on after painting, and we will fix it in place only after that stage, and then only with a spot of glue.

The pull rod that is supplied with the kit is etched and is intended to have the lower beams slotted through it. If such a pull rod is used then by all means fit it before painting. While it will restrict independent movement of the brake assemblies, provided that it is not fixed to any other point of the chassis it will still allow enough movement to permit the wheels to be fitted after placement.

As I mentioned earlier, I tend to use brass rod rather than etched components for these beams, although there are also good cast ones available that can be used, provided by some kits. I use another length of brass rod to represent the pull rods, where none is provided in the kit. Don't forget that the worm and gear or gearbox will protrude below the line of the axle and therefore more often than not the pull rod will need to be arranged to ensure that this is avoided.

Opposite top Prime and spray the chassis after removing the wheels and put it away for a day or so to let the paint harden. Here we see the chassis stripped and primed ready to be reassembled. Note that the plungers and springs need to be fitted before the wheels; do them one at a time as you are fitting the wheels. I assemble one wheel on each axle and, prior to inserting the axle into the chassis, fit a plunger and spring. Make sure the plunger moves easily and freely, and be careful not to lose the springs!

As the axle is pushed into the chassis the plunger is depressed. The axle is then held in place and the second plunger (at the other end of the axle) is positioned, followed by the other wheel. When this has been completed, ensuring that all cranks are at the same angle on each side but at 90 degrees to the opposite side, you can again check the freeness of the running, add the coupling rod and check again before finally fixing the rods in place and trimming the crank pins. With milled rods and chassis components such as those used here, it is unusual for there to be any problems with the chassis binding if it has been assembled carefully and accurately.

I should have mentioned of course that one axle will need also to go through a gear cradle or box and a gear wheel. It is common for gears to be fixed by a tiny grub screw to the axle. This use of a grub screw on a round surface such as an axle is not sound engineering practice as it gives minimum purchase.

This can be remedied by filing a flat surface on the axle and ensuring that the grub screw is tightened on to this.

Finally you need to connect the pick-ups to the motor, with the wire down each side connected to one of the terminals on the motor. Try to use the finest multi-strand wire you can get - I try to use black as it is less obvious if seen between the frames - and try to ensure that you solder it to the end surface of the pick-up, minimising interference on the action of the pick-up.

Then, hopefully, away we go. A very light lubrication of gears is beneficial and the merest spot of oil adjacent the wheel bearings will help smooth the early action of the chassis. However, be prepared to 'run in' the chassis for some time to get a smooth performance. It you don't have a continuous circuit to leave the model lapping around, try bench running.

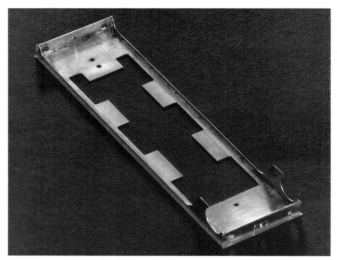

Now on to the footplate. The first stage is to fix the valances in place. Having been building models for many years I will, having ensured that there are no burrs on the edges of the valance, tack solder it in place, check that it is square and, when happy, run a fillet of solder along.

However, one dodge you can use to help this process is to solder a piece of brass angle to the footplate, then solder the valance to this. This gives the valance some strength - very helpful with the deep valances of earlier locomotives - and ensures that the valance is at 90 degrees to the footplate. Brass angle is readily available at model shops and at exhibitions, but ensure that it is shallow enough to be hidden behind your valance. It doesn't have to be the same depth and, in fact, it is usually more beneficial if it is only about half the depth of the valance to preserve the thinness of the edge.

The bufferbeams can now be added to this, but before you

do so, ensure that your buffer housings can be fixed in the holes provided in the beams. Invariably they need to be opened out and this is easier done by file or drill before assembly. I find it helpful to solder the buffer housings in place at this stage.

Bottom right You should by now have a square footplate on which to assemble the superstructure of the model. This kit has a rather novel and very useful arrangement to ensure the accurate alignment and assembly of the smokebox, boiler and firebox by means of machined formers that bolt together, enabling accurate soldering. The bolts are then removed to enable the firebox to be clear to accommodate the motor. These photographs show clearly the arrangement of the assembly and the components that make it up. The smokebox is soldered at its

base to a brass foundation block, which should have a nut soldered to it to enable the assembly to be bolted in place and accurately located, or, as in this case, the hole tapped 8BA. However, before fixing this assembly in place it will be found easier to fix the splashers.

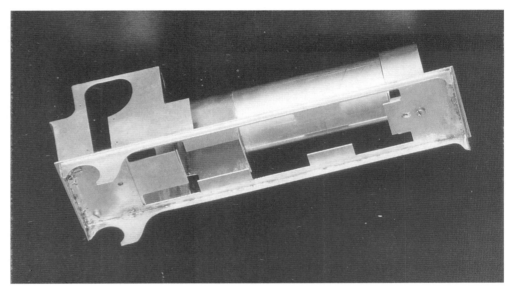

Left, below and opposite top The splashers are made from several separate components - sides and tops - and are a straightforward soldering job. It is easier, however, if they are assembled with simple jigs like the one shown in the diagram, using pins and a screwdriver

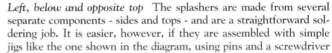

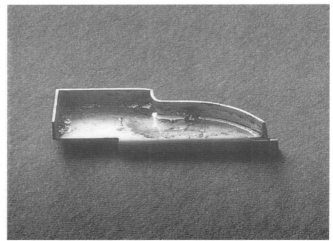

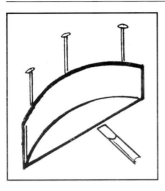

head to hold the pre-bent top in place while it is soldered to the side. Use of a lower-melting-point solder to fix the splashers to the footplate will minimise the risk of these sub-assemblies coming apart.

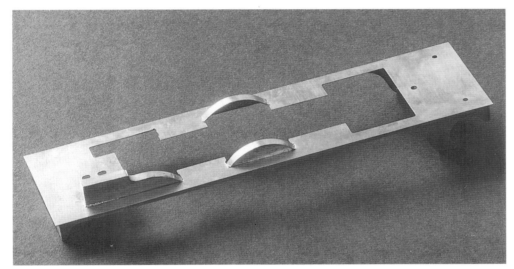

Below left and right The cab-sides and bunker back parts should be tried for fit, particularly checking the curve of the bunker back and if necessary manipulating it to ensure that it matches the profile of the sides. The bunker back of these locos had very distinctive rivets and these will need to be punched in from the half-etch holes on the inside. I will usually assemble the main shape before adding the detail such as the beading and coal rails.

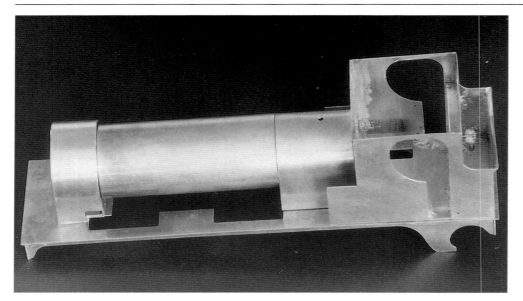

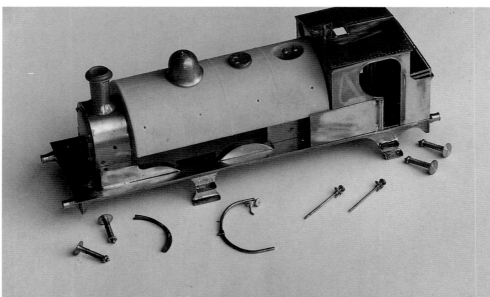

Top left The cab, firebox and boiler assembled on the footplate.

Middle left The reason for completing the chassis first is to ensure that the body does not foul it - it is much easier to modify a body than a chassis. The first stage should be to check that the footplate has the necessary clearance to avoid fouling wheels and motor by placing it on the chassis in the correct alignment, using the body locating holes as a guide, then holding the alignment in place while checking takes place.

When you are happy with the fit, solder in place the nuts that will hold the body to the chassis via the screws inserted from below through the frame spacers. I screw a nut and bolt tightly through this hole and, using the flux sparingly, solder the nut to the footplate, ensuring that the nut does not get soldered to the bolt! In this kit the milled base of the smokebox is tapped and drilled both to secure it to the footplate and to the chassis. In this shot we are also checking clearance and fit of other sub-assemblies on the footplate.

Bottom left The 'plumbing' needs to be considered next, and the holes in the resin water tanks for the injector and balance pipes need to be opened out to ensure that the necessary parts will fit correctly.

Before you fit the tanks, fit the handrails on the footplate above the forward steps, the valve covers, lamp brackets adjacent to the firebox - used for storing spare lamps - and solder the steps to the valance. The boiler bands on these locos are not visible unless you squint below the tank, but if you want to fit them, do so before the tank is added. The tank is glued in place on the boiler.

The chimney, dome and safety valves are glued in place. You may need to spend a bit of time with a file and wet and dry to ensure that

they fit well - gaping holes between chimney base and smokebox or a leaning chimney immediately jar on the eye, so a bit of
care here is well rewarded. With final details applied, the locomotive is then ready for the paint shop.

Right A rare and invaluable detail view of the safety valves and
tank top of a prototype saddle tank loco.

Above and right One method
of achieving a removable cab
roof has already been
described - here is another.
The cab roof has a false part-
front and rear soldered to the
underside, which form a push
fit on to the cab front and
rear. This enables the interior
to be detailed.

To complete the cab the
beading, ventilator and whis-
tle need to be applied. The
splashers and bunker front
are soldered up as part of the
main cab construction, but
the cast firebox back is
detailed, with the pipework,
gauges, regulator handle, etc,
fitted. It can be painted separately and added, courtesy of
your removable roof, after
the main body is painted.

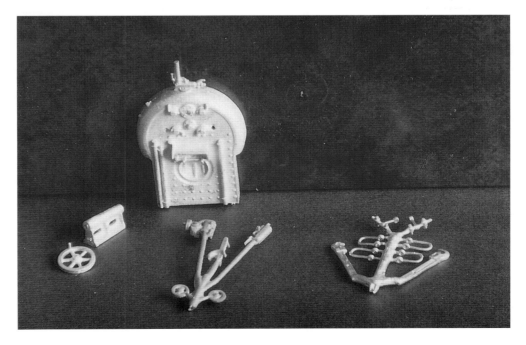

Fowler 2-6-2T No 40058

These locomotives began to appear in 1930 and were an attempt to fill the need for an intermediate passenger locomotive. They followed the development of established 'Midland' practice using the basic 8 ft x 8 ft 6 in coupled wheelbase, adapted cylinders and valve gear from the Somerset & Dorset 2-8-0s, and boilers developed from the Fowler '2F' 0-6-0 but with superheating. They had, not surprisingly, a distinctive 'Midland' look about them. Ultimately 70 were built, of which 28 were fitted with condensing apparatus to work the London area 'Widened Lines'.

Despite being a relatively small class - LMS classes more commonly numbered into the hundreds, particularly in the Stanier era - there were several detail variations, notwithstanding the aforementioned condensing gear. These detail variations can be summarised as flush or snaphead rivets to the tank and bunker, small or large frame extensions (the vertical bits above the lower footplate), plain or fluted coupling rods, and outside or inside steam pipes, while some were motor-fitted for push-pull working.

As there were only 70 of these locomotives and so many variations, I have attempted to summarise them in the accompanying table. All the class eventually received, from 1945 onwards, outside steampipes and replacement cylinders and a large-diameter, lower chimney. Note that this modification resulted in the chimney being aligned further forward on the smokebox to align with the steampipes and centre of the cylinder.

| Locomotive number | | | | |
Original	1934 number	Date built	Variations	Comments
15500-19	1-20	1930	Small frame extension, non-condensing, fluted coupling rods	Nos 10, 12 and 17 motor-fitted in 1937, '47 and '54 respectively
15520-24	21-25	1930	Small frame extension, condensing, fluted coupling rods	No 20 motor-fitted in 1935, No 21 lost its condensing gear in 1944
15525-39	26-40	1931	Large frame extension, condensing, fluted coupling rods	
15540-49	41-50	1931	Large frame extension, non-condensing	No 45 motor-fitted in 1954
15550-59	51-60	1931/32	Large frame extension, non-condensing	Nos 56 onwards motor-fitted in 1939, No 58 only until 1947
15560-69	61-70	1932	'Stanier' period build with plain coupling rods, snaphead rivets and balance weights	No 61 motor-fitted in 1939

Notes

For BR numbers add 40,000 to the 1934 number: eg No 58 became 40058.
Withdrawal began in 1959, the last locos going in 1962.

This is No 15524, one of the 1930 batch of Fowler 2-6-2Ts with condensing gear, which basically consisted of the condensing pipes linking smokebox to tank and Weir feed pump (opposite side). Initially, as with many other LMS classes built around this period, the rear carrying wheels were fitted with brakes - a feature quickly removed by Stanier. This photograph shows clearly the original LMS livery with single red lining and yellow-shaded red insignia. *R. J. Essery*

Top right Our loco, No 58, showing the conversion with outside steam pipes and wider chimney, but still in LMS livery. *R. J. Essery*

Middle right 2-6-2T No 40014 at Bolton in 1959, a loco from the original batch in, save for the BR emblem on the tank side, its last BR condition with outside steam pipes. Its condition is fairly typical - they were not popular. *Author's collection*

Bottom right The construction of the Chowbent Castings kit covers the same basic principles established earlier with the 0-6-0 saddle tank. Accordingly I will not go over the same ground, but rather concentrate on the differences and aspects that were not encountered on the previous loco, for example cylinders and valve gear.

This view shows the basic frame/cylinder assembly. This chassis is like the previous one in that it is etched in brass and requires bolting together. The chassis requires a deal more work than the last we encountered, because of the outside cylinders and motion brackets, but if the sequence suggested in the instructions is followed and sufficient time taken, then there should be little problem.

The chassis will be surprisingly strong when assembled, the cylinder and other transverse motion-related components giving it rigidity and providing a solid base for the outside valve gear. Spend a bit of time ensuring that the components slot in accurately, and don't force components into slots or the chassis will be distorted. Once again use the plate glass to help ensure a level base on which to work.

If you are going to compensate or spring the chassis you need to determine this before

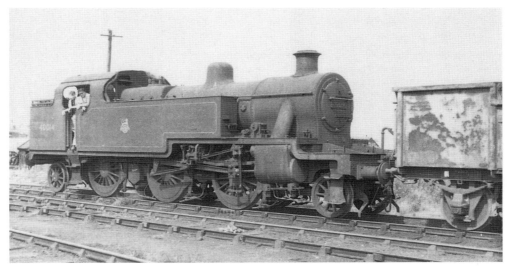

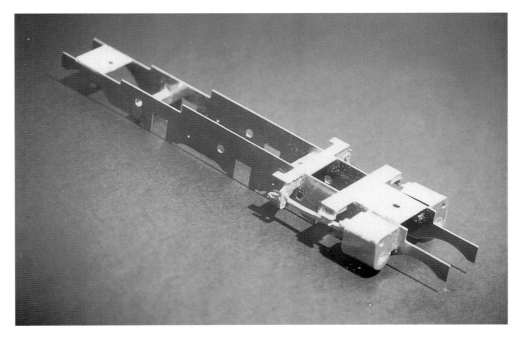

you begin assembly as you will need to remove a section of the side frames. As already mentioned, I have mixed views on the question of compensation. However, on all larger six-coupled locomotives I will invariably open up the centre hole in the chassis to allow the wheel bearing a little vertical movement. This helps no end in avoiding the chassis rocking on the centre driver on high spots in trackwork, such as crossing vees and rail joints. Half a millimetre or so is all that is required. However, be very careful to ensure that there is no horizontal movement, or the chassis will not work as in essence you will have altered the wheelbase.

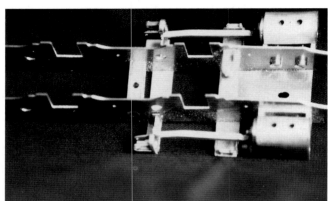

Above right and right Two further views of the cylinder and motion bracket assembly on the frames. The accurate assembly of these is essential to the running of the finished chassis. The holes at the base of the cylinder are for the cylinder drain cocks, supplied as a casting. The cylinder wrappers are wrapped around milled formers as in the smokebox and firebox encountered with the saddle tank. The slots in the frames are to accommodate Slaters hornblocks to enable the finished loco to be sprung.

Left The frames in place. The motion bracket will have suspended from it the reversing and combination levers of the Walschaerts valve gear. The bar running between cylinder and motion bracket, also supported on the motion bracket, is the slide bar on which the crosshead will run, enabling the rod to move the piston valve within the cylinder. Accurate alignment is essential.

Below left Like the saddle tank and the Aspinall 0-6-0 goods loco, this kit also has milled components to help assembly and accurate location of the smokebox, boiler and firebox. Note the additional detail along the top of the boiler, with a line scored to represent the join in the boiler cladding and the rivets formed from short lengths of wire soldered into pre-drilled holes and filed to length. This was done by Bob Lomax who built No 40070 seen later. This sort of detail lifts a model just that bit above the ordinary.

The bunker, cab and tank sides soldered on the footplate around the cab front and rear. Note the rivet detail along the edge of the footplate, and that the buffers have been added at this stage.

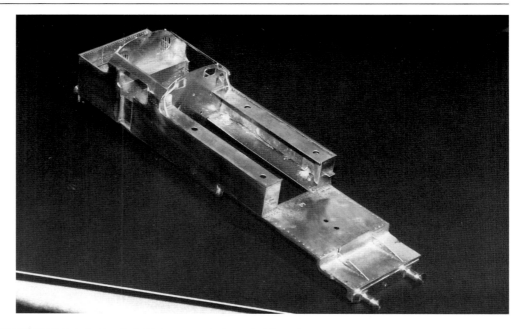

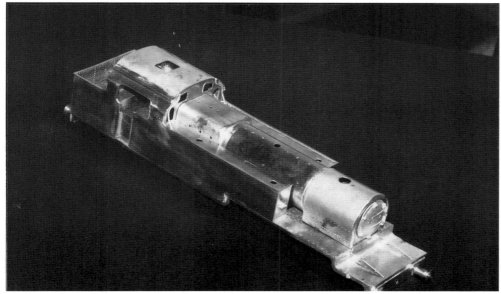

The basic loco body is now together with smokebox, boiler and firebox in place and cab roof fitted. Now is the time to add details prior to a visit to the paint shop.

Wire guards over the cab rear windows were a common feature of many tank locos to protect against breakage when coaling. If no casting or etching is supplied the bars can easily be fabricated by soldering wire, pre-bent, into pre-drilled holes. The bunker, rear steps and handrail have also been added. The beading is a flat etch, therefore accurately pre-shaped to ease the sweating-on process.

The basic body shell on the frames. The design of this Chowbent kit, with the use of sprung hornblocks, enables the motion to be disconnected and the loco lifted from its wheels, frames, cylinders and all, as on the prototype.

A close-up view of the finished locomotive showing the accurate appearance and feel achieved by the level of detail supplied in the kit. The lubricators have been drilled and feed pipe added, otherwise the detail is largely 'lost wax' brass detail castings whose quality shines through to give that elusive 'feel'.

As they say in a certain television programme, here's one I made earlier! This is not the Platt Lane loco but another built in exactly the same way from a Chowbent kit by Bob Lomax. No 40070 is seen here shunting at Platt Lane.

Fairburn 2-6-4T No 42119

This locomotive, despite being a tank locomotive, is quite large. The class was essentially a post-Second World War development of the Stanier 2-6-4 tank locomotives built in 1935. They basically updated Stanier's locomotives, which had been, and indeed continued to be, very successful, incorporating later developments in locomotive design and, by reducing the coupled wheelbase from the 16 ft 6 in of the Stanier locomotives to 15 ft 4 in the 'new' version, achieved a greater route availability, which was also enhanced by a weight reduction.

Externally they showed little variation from their forefathers except for the cut-away of the drop footplate in front of the cylinders, a shallower section footplate and the use of open strap steps in place of the earlier solid platesteps. The locomotives, 277 of which were built, performed a wide range of duties from branch and local services to semi-fast expresses. They also strayed widely, being common not only in the North West but also working the Glasgow suburban and Clyde Coast services, appearing on the Southend line and in North East England.

Forty-one of the class, Nos 42066-42106, were built at Brighton in 1951 and were used until the late 1950s on the Southern Region where they were allocated to the Central Division and performed similar duties to their sisters elsewhere. These Southern Region-based locomotives were later drafted to the London, Midland, North Eastern and Scottish Regions, and were replaced by the later development of the same type, the BR Standard 2-6-4Ts.

No 42119 was based at Springs Branch shed, Wigan (8G), in 1959, and is typical of the kind of motive power used on local passenger, van and parcel trains in the area at this time.

She will be primarily used on Platt Lane to haul the Manchester service and, as built for the layout, will represent a locomotive in lined BR mixed traffic livery, albeit rather grubby, of which more later.

I chose the DJH kit from which to produce

the model because it brings into our consideration a further type of kit that uses the etched brass chassis previously encountered, but has a cast white metal boiler, smokebox and firebox and etched brass tank sides. It also uses the more common double-slide-bar Walschaerts valve gear.

The valve gear does not employ milled components, but rather the individual rods are soldered up from etched nickel parts. These often need to be sweated together to get a suitable thickness on the heavier rods, for example the coupling and con-rods. Most of the coupling rods provided of this type allow for the rod to be jointed, which is essential if your locomotive is sprung or compensated, otherwise the rod will prevent the axles from moving up and down in their guides.

This type of valve gear construction can be fiddly, particularly on the smaller rods as they have to be lined up perfectly and have clean holes to allow them to be connected to the next piece. Another unusual feature of the valve gear is that it is arranged prototypically to be opened out to provide the correct type of joint - one component fitted in the slotted end of the other.

This kit is designed so that the front dropped footplate section is assembled on the frames; the footplate is dropped in the cab and bunker area. Where this type of footplate is encountered great care needs to be taken to ensure that it is squarely and accurately assembled. Accordingly I always use a simple jig made from scrap timber that will hold the higher part at the correct level. It is essential in virtually all British model locomotives that the footplate is squarely and accurately assembled, as this forms the basis of the locomotive body. Consequently any inaccuracies at this stage will be magnified as the superstructure develops.

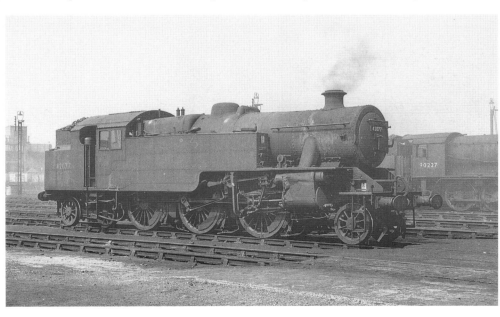

A superb view of Fairburn 2-6-4T No 42077 in fairly typical condition in 1959. Note the steps, front footplate and other minor details differentiating these locos from their Stanier predecessors. *D. Hampson*

Top left A Stanier 2-6-4T on a Blackburn-Bolton train approaching Entwistle in 1960. Compare this loco with the Fairburn shown in the previous picture for detail differences. *D. Hampson*

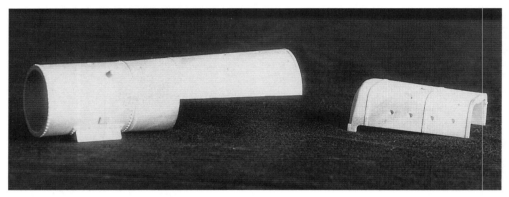

Middle left The smokebox, boiler and firebox in this kit are cast in white metal, which makes assembly easier, not least because much of the detail is cast in. It is quite possible to solder white metal components using a low-melt solder and a small low-heat iron. However, in this particular case I chose to use 'superglue'. Before the parts are assembled you will need to clean up the components, remove any moulding flash, etc, and clean the metal where it is to be glued.

As always it is essential to ensure that they are accurately aligned and that the top of these assemblies is at the top and the locating holes central - otherwise when you add the chimney and dome you will have difficulty getting them on without a lean!

The other main body components fit on to the footplate quite easily with slot and tab. Ensure that these are squarely assembled before proceeding. The tank sides are unusual in that like the prototype they have an inside, or back. One advantage of this is that not only does it give more detail and faithfulness to the real thing, despite being hidden, but it adds strength to the large expanse of metal that is commonly the place where we hold the model when we pick it up. It thus helps prevent any damage through the tank sides being squashed.

Bottom left A DJH Fairburn tank loco complete and painted, ready for the road. This is not the Platt lane loco, but is included to show what the finished model should look like on completion after a hefty dose of weathering. This loco was again made by **Bob Lomax**.

Aspinall Class '27' 0-6-0 goods No 52447

These famous locomotives were the second type to be built at the then new Horwich Locomotive Works in 1891, and their success is exemplified by both their longevity (the saturated round-top boiler types, as on our model, only going in 1961), and by their wide distribution over the LMS system, from London to Wales, straying far from their homeland.

They formed the largest group of L&YR 0-6-0 engines absorbed by the LMS and were numbered by the LMS in the 12083 to 12467 series. They were effectively an Aspinall development of the earlier Barton-Wright 0-6-0 goods locomotives. The class was to be built over a 30-year period and, not surprisingly, contained some modifications, the principal of which were the building of some with Belpaire fireboxes and others with superheated boilers.

Other more minor modifications concerned the replacement of the earlier taper chimney, common along with many other parts with the 2-4-2 passenger tanks, with a parallel type, the replacement of Ramsbottom safety valves with Ross 'pop' valves, and the replacement of lighter taper buffers, albeit gradually, with a parallel type.

The original smoke-box door was fixed with a centre door fastening and because of warpage this was later superseded by a series of clamps or 'dogs' around the perimeter. These replacement doors also had a slightly different profile and contained a short separate length of handrail, in contrast to the continuous handrail of the earlier types.

A Platt Lane-style Aspinall 0-6-0 shunting at Bolton in 1960. Note the general appearance, something that I have tried to copy on the Platt Lane loco, Lower Darwen-based No 52447 seen in the second photograph.

Eventually there were 496 0-6-0s in their various guises. The story of their modification is complex, many earlier engines being rebuilt with Belpaire boilers in both superheated and saturated form. The superheated boilers were introduced in 1913, two years after the Belpaire fireboxes. Superheated locos are generally recognised by the chimney being forward on the smokebox, but the majority of superheated locomotives sported extended smokeboxes with the chimney in the original position. Extended front splashers and a slightly different cab also resulted from this modification.

As with all locomotives built in large numbers with several permutations of modifications, a photograph is essential. However, with L&Y locomotives there is also the late Eric Mason's exceptional work *The L&Y in the 20th Century*, which documents much of this change.

The model is built from a Chowbent Castings kit, which comprises an etched brass superstructure and milled brass chassis and rods. The smokebox, firebox

and boiler bolt together on formers as did the saddle tank and Fowler loco.

The splashers, being etched, are a little different from those on the saddle tank; their basic assembly is essentially in two stages, folding up the sides from the footplate and soldering the tops in place. This can be a bit fiddly, but carefully pre-shaping the tops to the profile of the sides helps.

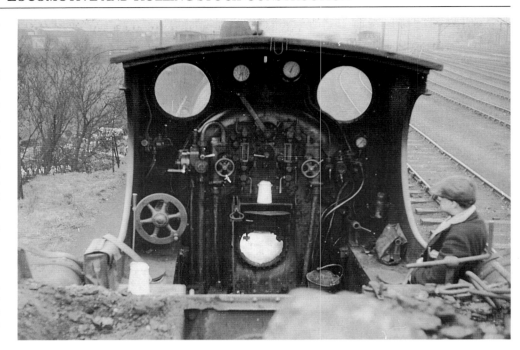

A cab interior of an Aspinall 0-6-0, invaluable for modelling! You really have to model the interiors of these open cabs.

The chassis for the Aspinall is a simple bolt-together assembly and accordingly I have shown a completed example, primed, from a Chowbent kit.

The basic formers and components for the smokebox, firebox and boiler follow the same principles in the Chowbent Aspinall as in the saddle tank and Fowler 2-6-2 tank.

The rest of the superstructure is a straightforward soldering operation, but because the cab is open and conspicuous a good deal of care needs to be taken to ensure that it is clearly detailed with screw reverse, backhead and detail, and the rear sandbox levers. Note the painted-in dials and that the original short L&Y regulator lever was extended by the LMS in the 1930s, a feature that continued until scrapping and one easily represented by cutting and shaping a piece of scrap material from the etch frets and fixing in place. This is a view of an L&Y period model.

Right It is worthwhile adding a bit of detail such as the supports, couplings and gubbins on the vacuum brake pipework, as has been done here. It is surprising what you can do with washers, wire and a bit of scrap metal. Note also the loco springs fixed inside the frames.

Below Paint adds detail and character, as in the brakes and wheels of No 52447 seen here.

Top left This is the first time that we have encountered a tender. This kit provides for quite a detailed model and, while generally a straightforward box, it has some complications that I felt it would be useful to illustrate. Here we see the basic tender underframe.

Middle left Tenders are basically a box to which further detail is added, and in themselves rarely cause a problem. It is when we start adding to the box that problems occur, for example in applying flared tender tops. The flare has to be bent out by the builder and there are two approaches. One is to bend the tops carefully around a piece of bar - a piece of Meccano rod is ideal - then add them to the tender sides, manipulating and filing the joint with the back flare to get a correct fit and running a fillet of solder down the inside of the joint.

The second method is to solder the sides and back unbent into the half-etched tops of the sides, then to bend them outwards from the top over the steel rod. What you are looking for is a gentle large-radius bend to almost 90 degrees outwards from bottom to top.

It sounds a bit fiddly - and it is - but it is easier to do than to explain. As usual you need to proceed with care, going for even bends along the whole length of the flare. You will find that, because it is deeper, the rear end of the side will tend to curve more easily. However, you must ensure an even bend and put more effort into the front to keep things even. What you want to avoid is a flare with lots of dimples and different bends, although a few slight deviations may be acceptable as the tops would receive a battering under coal hoppers!

When you have put the flares on you have done the hardest part of the model. The addition of the coal rails is relatively straightforward. Simply bend the legs around a piece of rod to match the tops of the flairs, then tin and solder them in place. Note that you will need to bend down the front of the coal rails and solder them in place.

Once this has been done and all the soldering cleaned up, the detail castings and fittings can be fixed in place. Cast axleboxes and etched tender steps are fabricated as those on the saddle tank.

Bottom left Extra detail is not just confined to the loco - for example, pinheads provide tool box cupboard handles. The cab fallplate provided in the kit can be made to pivot by the simple expedient of soldering a piece of fine tube to the rear underside and running through this some wire that has its ends bent at 90 degrees and soldered into pre-drilled holes in the draw-beam. The tender hook needs to be nothing more elaborate than a hook made from brass wire fitting into a loop made from bent wire.

Right No 52447 shunting the Platt Lane coal drops.

LMS '4F' 0-6-0 tender loco No 44317

No 44317 was chosen to represent the '4F' on the layout. It was in 1959 a Sutton Oak loco and worked a number of services, principally freight, in the area.

These locomotives originated on the Midland Railway, which was, so far as freight traffic was concerned, an 0-6-0 line *par excellence*, operating with a view that more frequent trains and double-heading were preferable to bigger locos; strange when you consider the 2-8-0s built for the Somerset & Dorset. However, despite a common coupled wheelbase of 8 ft to 8 ft 6 in, Midland 0-6-0s existed in bewildering variety.

The Class '4s', or 'big goods', which I suppose they were by Midland standards, were the culmination of 0-6-0 goods loco development on the Midland and appeared in 1911 to the design of Henry Fowler. They became an early standard type for the LMS and were built until 1941, the LMS building 575 examples and the Midland 197.

The LMS-built examples were primarily right-hand drive and were built without beading on the splashers. Other detail differences concerned chimneys (several types were used), the removal of tail rod housings with consequent cover plates on the front buffer beam on earlier examples, while later versions had shorter rods requiring no external housings outside the curtilage of the frames, and of course tenders. A whole chapter could be devoted to the permutations, not least in respect of tenders. Photographs are definitely necessary when modelling '4Fs'.

The model is built from an Alan Gibson kit, which provides not only a wide selection of alternative parts to cover most common varieties, but can be specified

with either a Fowler 3,500-gallon or earlier Johnson-type tender. A selection of number plates is also provided, but alas not the one we needed.

The wheels used are Alan Gibson's own design and provide a different approach from the Slaters wheels used earlier, incorporating 'telescopic' axles fitted with a locking pin. They have turned steel rims that are fitted on cast centres, insulated at the boss.

The body is basically of a similar pattern of assembly to the earlier locos described, except that there are no bolt-together formers for firebox and smokebox. These have to be formed carefully, particularly the Belpaire firebox; the brass is quite thin and the front and rear formers are suitable only for holding in place, not for bending around! I find that they are an essential grind, but that the bending of sides and tops needs to be done around something substantial.

Place the firebox wrapper down flat, and the former flat but butted up to the front of the wrapper, in the correct position. Mark the centre line of the wrapper and former carefully and accurately, then mark the top and lower edge of the curve at the top edge of the firebox. Using a piece of Meccano rod, and with constant reference to the former, begin to shape the bend. Ensure that the top is kept flat and that the bend is straight and even. Solder this in place on the inside of the former.

A similar process is involved in bending up the cab. This is slightly more complex than the firebox in that the cab side is cut away from the rear so you end up with plenty of metal to bend at the front of the side but little for the rear half. Be careful, take your time and use the rod again, ensuring a straight, even bend.

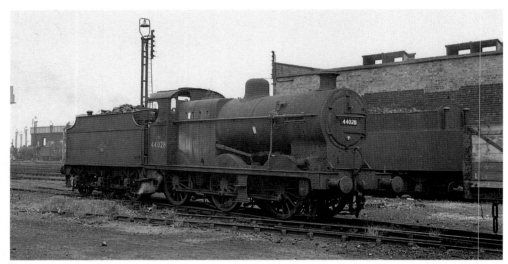

Top and middle In common with many so-called standard locos built over a period, '4Fs' had a great many variations, complicated by the Midland and LMS building batches and even BR adding modifications. *D. Hampson*

This locomotive is also a new departure for our stock as it is fully sprung with hornblocks provided. There is nothing really complicated about assembling these - follow the instructions and be patient. This shows the assembly of the hornblocks into the chassis.

The tender for our No 44317 is a Fowler 3,500-gallon type and as such has a few features different from those encountered

with the Aspinall, but fortunately no tender flares to bend up! These pictures show the main features of the construction.

Alternative locos - a pair of Ivatts

In the earlier section on locomotive choice I mentioned a number of possible alternatives and permutations in the locos we could use on Platt Lane. Here therefore I will briefly outline the Ivatt Class '2' tank and tender locos, not least because we will have the tender loco on Platt Lane.

As has become usual so far, I will start with a few notes on the prototypes. The 2-6-2T and 2-6-0 tender locomotives were essentially variants of the same, carrying common components; essentially the former was a tank version of the slightly earlier 2-6-0 tender loco. They were both rather interesting in being part of a novel policy of building new locos for secondary duties. They incorporated the latest thinking, albeit based firmly on the now well-established LMS practice, and were intended to have wide route availability and be competent on a wide range of duties. Both types were perpetuated in modified form in the BR Standard designs.

The tank locos began to appear at the end of 1946,

originally designated Class '2' but becoming Class '2MT' in 1948. Several of the class, Nos 41210-29, 41270-89 and 41320-29, were motor-fitted from new to run push-pull services, but not all retained this feature.

Many of the class worked on the Southern Region from the late 1950s, and these locomotives acquired an additional front lamp bracket for the Southern headcode discs, but these were not always removed from locos returning to the LMR. There were also three distinct types of chimneys fitted to these locomotives. As well as being widely spread on the LMR and Southern Regions, there was a smattering on other Regions.

No 41287 is the locomotive chosen for Platt Lane and was motor-fitted, being therefore ideal for our push-pull service. Like most of her sisters she was well travelled, but in the period with which we are concerned she flitted between Patricroft and Sutton Oak.

The model was built from a Wigan Wagon Works kit, as was the 2-6-0 tender loco. The kit is etched brass and its design includes the rivets, beading, boiler bands and other surface detail etched on the appropriate component and thus, for me, saves a lot of time and avoids the possible difficulties caused by warping a tank side if you have to punch out dozens of rivets.

Top right A push-pull-fitted Ivatt at Great Moor Street in 1951. Note the push-pull detail on the smokebox and the modified steam pipes. These can be fabricated from wire and scrap material by reference to photographs. So far as I am aware at the time of writing, no 7 mm scale kits are available for this gear as fitted to the Ivatt. *Author's collection*

Middle right The basic chassis is etched, cross-members locating the frames. The cylinder front and back traverse the frames and are slotted in. Don't force their fit - they should be tight but not so tight as to distort the frames. Otherwise construction follows the pattern set earlier.

Bottom right The basic tank loco and chassis showing the detailed casting added to the etched components. The spring detail is etched into the chassis; the marks round the axle holes are half-etch lines to enable easy, accurate removal of metal to fit hornblocks if you want springing. The cylinder wrappers are castings, saving the need to sweat on brass wrappers.

For the first time we encounter a taper boiler and the more traditional methods of making model boilers by soldering a wrapper around a ring. Here the smokebox is tackled first, on end, the ring soldered in place from the inside and the wrapper held in place with a binding of wire around the outside, which is later cut free.

The ring at the other end must be soldered from the outside, but with the former inset by 1 mm to allow the outer ring in which the smokebox door fits to be placed just proud by a whisker from the smokebox ring. This ring can be glued or soldered in place with low-melt solder. The outer edge should be very lightly chamfered - just run a piece of wet and dry around it a couple of times.

The taper boiler is formed in exactly the same way, but ensure that you put the right former at the right end - the larger towards the firebox.

These two assemblies can be fixed together with Araldite or low-melt solder by carefully trimming both outer edges and holding a hot iron near and long enough to fuse the low-melt but not the ordinary solder used on the smokebox and boiler. Make sure that, if anything, one ring is slightly - a whisker only - inset from the edge.

When fitting the firebox to the locomotive, note that it should be slightly lower at the cab end. The curved front corners are achieved by means of a casting that forms the firebox front.

The type of bunker on these locomotives is inset to allow good views when travelling bunker first. You will have to form the upper portions of the bunker yourself; it is a bit fiddly, but using the bunker back as a guide, a matter of patient manipulation rather than difficulty.

Finished Ivatt 2-6-2 tank No 41240.

Ivatt 2-6-0 No 46428 was built in 1948 and was a Wigan Springs Branch loco from 1954 to 1962. She would therefore be an appropriate choice for Platt Lane and could cover anything from semi-fast passenger and van trains to trip freights.

This model is a Wigan Wagon Works kit and follows the basic style of design and construction of the tank loco. Here the model is nearing completion, and the paint shop beckons!

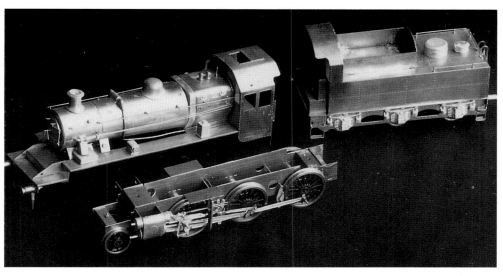

The steam chests will, and the pipes may, need filling to get a good fit. The steam chests (the boxes above the footplate over the cylinder) have been left with square ends enabling them to be filed to fit rather than have the difficulty of filling or an unsightly gap in an inaccessible place, as it is quite possible that you may not all get the smokebox saddle sides at the same angle.

Top left The footplate is different as it has no inset or deep valance, but a shallow flush one. This is formed on the kit by folding over the edge along a half-etched line on the underside. This presents no problem on the short length on the tank side, but on the long stretch on the tender loco a bit of care is needed. Long bending bars would be helpful, but a good solid surface and a long substantial steel ruler will do the trick.

Middle left The cab assembly is based around the footplate and cab front. The method of assembly, soldering from the inside, is clearly seen. The key thing is to ensure that the cab is vertical.

Middle right The tender, like the others, is a basic box, and while it has no coal rails or flares to the sides, it has a tender cab. This is simply made by first bending the cab roof to the profile of the back before soldering it in place. The tender rear steps (and the bunker steps on the tank loco) are, if you attempting to get something that looks like the real thing on a model, a pain!

Bottom left The completed model prior to painting.

Painting and lining locomotives

I should perhaps start by saying that once the model is cleaned and prepared for painting it should be handled as little as possible. However, there is an obvious need to move the locomotive around while spraying to achieve an even coat, and I use an improvised spray booth comprising a cardboard box with the top and front cut away, and a can or pot lid placed on the base; this much be tall and strong enough to support the model and allow it to be turned without touching the model itself.

Perhaps the most common colour for locomotives is black, and here again recourse to car touch-up aerosol is made. Matt black touch-up paint is used, even in O gauge, as a high gloss finish just does not look right on small-scale models. This matt black paint actually has a slight sheen to it if applied under normal temperature conditions, in my view just about right for our models.

There are other advantages too in using this paint. In particular, being cellulose based it dries very hard and is touch dry within minutes, thus minimising contamination from that old enemy, dust. Lining can be carried out with enamel paints and any unsatisfactory work removed without damaging the cellulose base colour. It is, however, essential to use this paint in a well-ventilated room, or better still outside, and away from any naked flame or heating elements.

The primed model should now be examined closely, but again handled as little as possible, and any imperfections in the surface dealt with now. The primer will show up imperfections better than the unprimed surface did, as there is no reflection to deflect our critical eye. Remember that whatever imperfections you see now, particularly dust and excess glue or solder not cleaned away, will show up even worse when the top coat is applied.

When you are happy with the finish, consideration can be given to the final coat. The choice of livery is clearly up to the builder and, if earlier advice on choosing to model a particular loco at a given period was followed, no doubt the livery will probably have been determined by how the model was detailed. There is now so much information available that major inaccuracies are inexcusable, even though there may be some doubt about the finer details of liveries.

There are well-matched paints for a significant number of railway colours available in aerosol cans and in small tinlets that can be thinned for an airbrush. Alternatively, that good old stand-by the car aerosol touch-up paint is available in such a wide range of colours that a fair approximation of the colour needed is almost certainly available. There is also now the excellent Rail Match range, which is colour matched to the principal colours of British railway liveries.

Colour perception is a very personal matter and it's your model, so it's important that you're happy that the colour you've chosen. If you use the matched paints then this problem should not arise.

Without doubt the best finish is obtained with an airbrush, and if you are going to build a lot of kits it is a worthwhile investment. I have to be honest and admit to favouring the aerosol can, even though I have both airbrush and spray gun. I wouldn't recommend brush painting locomotives other than for small areas as it is difficult to get a finish comparable to a sprayed one.

Whether you use an airbrush or an aerosol, the basic techniques are the same. Light, even coats are required, building up the finish stage by stage rather than trying to cover in one coat. Keep the can at a reasonable distance from the model and move the spray evenly and horizontally along the length of the model. It is of paramount importance that the spray is kept moving and not allowed to stop at all, otherwise an uneven coating will result. Start the movement just before and finish it just after the model.

Buffer beams can be painted with a brush and matt paint. Ensure that any paint is thoroughly stirred before use and is applied in thin, even coats from a good quality, clean, preferably sable, brush. Similarly other detail can be painted and - in other than black locos, the smokebox and footplate, splasher tops, etc.

If the model requires lining out, once the top coat and details are painted you can consider how best to achieve this. Basically it is a question of transfers or hand lining. It is of course essential that the paint on the model has hardened thoroughly before the lining and transfers are added. I prefer to put the model on one side for at least a week after painting, even with cellulose paint, placing it in a box to prevent dust getting to it.

Transfers come in a variety of colours and styles, covering the main liveries of British railway companies. They will be of two basic types, waterslide or the self-adhesive press-fix type, and should be applied in accordance with the manufacturer's recommendations. There are now a number of preparations available from your model shop to help transfers settle down over rivet and similar surface detail and to dissolve corner film on waterslide transfers. I find 4 mm scale lining transfers excellent in most cases for 7 mm scale applications, particularly the usually coarser waterslide type.

With waterslide transfers, despite suggestions on the instructions that it is not necessary, I have always carefully cut with a new, fine blade right up to the design or as near as practically possible. Waterslide transfers have the advantage of being easy to adjust and move - very useful with lining, particularly with boiler band lining, which will have to be slid under handrails and other details. For these it is easier to apply them if they are cut to length before soaking and taken to the model still on their carrying layer. Place them in the approximate position, then remove the carrying layer from beneath the design and adjusted the transfer to its final position.

Press-fix transfers are also easy to use and my preferred choice, although they cannot easily be adjusted and must be applied in their final position. This isn't an onerous task on plain sides, but where complicated curved or narrow edges need to be lined, such as footplate valances or wheel splashers, it is easier to cut the design from the sheet or to release it on to glass and then transfer it to the model. On panelling, such as tender sides, I mark the corners with a soft pencil, add the corner transfers first then fill in the straight lines.

You can still buy rub-on transfers, but beware that the paint doesn't peel from the surface as the transfer leaves the backing sheet. It helps to prevent this if the transfer is part released by rubbing over the backing sheet, thus starting the process before it is applied to the model.

Hand lining is by no means as difficult as it sounds and, like any other model work, practice is the key to good results. The draughtsman's spring bowpen is the best tool for the job and is not difficult to use; the technique has already been touched upon in the chapter on coaches. There is also a specialist lining pen now on the market that gives excellent results.

The spring of the bowpen is tightened to thin the line to be drawn, and slackened off to widen it. Only new paint should be used, thoroughly mixed and thinned if necessary, to a consistency that will allow it to flow from the pen evenly without flooding. The bowpen is tightened, paint added between the spring blades using a cocktail stick to a maximum of a quarter of an inch up the blades, then the blades are opened until the correct thickness of line is drawn - practise on scrap material. Lining can then commence on the model. The pen must be kept

The Fowler 2-6-2T in plain black primer, and fully painted and weathered with lining and numbers applied. Both models are by Bob Lomax.

vertical at all times to ensure an even flow of paint from the point of the blades. Try to finish a line with one fill of the pen rather than run out of paint halfway along; experience will show how much you can do with the paint left in the pen before it runs out. To refill the pen, clean it out thoroughly in thinners, stir the paint well and continue.

It is quite feasible to line large panels such as tender sides with the aid of a template. This can be cut from plasticard, the edges smoothed and the corners curved accurately if appropriate. It is then held in the correct position on the model with small bits of Blue-Tack in each corner and drawn round with a pen. Try the template out on scrap first to ensure the correct shape and that sufficient smoothness of edge has been achieved to let the pen pass round easily.

If you build a few models eventually a set of templates can be built up, and it is useful to label them - 'BR mixed traffic livery - red line Fowler 3,500 gallon tender side' - for future use. Multi-coloured lining can easily be built up using successively smaller templates, starting with the outside line first.

To line the model successfully it is important that it is held still and that there is some means of supporting the ruler when straight lines are drawn. The arrangement shown on page 59 is adequate for this purpose, or for 'one-off' jobs you could improvise with heavy books.

There are many lettering transfers available and their application calls for little comment other than to ensure that the rows of numbers and letters are applied level and vertical, not as easy or as obvious as it sounds. The best aid to this is a pencil base line.

When you are happy with the finish, a coat of varnish can be applied to protect the paint, lining and lettering. The aerosols available from Rail Match and Humbrol provide a range of alternative finishes, from dead matt to high gloss. I prefer a satin finish applied in light coats as previously discussed for the primer and top coat.

When painting the cab interior, usually the top half is a light buff or cream colour and the bottom half black or brown. Pick out the gauges and pipework in brass and copper, painting the faces of the gauges white.

Buffer heads should be dark grey with a dark smudged centre, and the shanks painted silver to represent the polished steel from the continual compression into their housings. However, if you have used buffers with steel heads you could remove them before painting and replace them afterwards. You can then dirty the heads to your pleasure and leave the shanks steel.

All that is now left is to add the finishing details such as coal in the tender or bunker - here there is no substitute for the real thing. I use crushed coal glued on to a piece of shaped sponge and held in place with slightly diluted PVA woodwork glue applied with an eye-dropper.

Also add lamps - there are several cast ones available from Springside, as are locomotive tool sets, fire irons, etc. Alternatively these tools can easily be fabricated from bits of left-over handrail wire and scrap material. Don't forget to add some spilt coal around the tender front footplate, near the coal plate or around the tender top near the water fillers. If you don't want lamps fixed to your loco, place some on the footplate; the GWR, for example, often had spare lamps carried on brackets there. Spare lamps might also be carried on the tender front near the lockers, and locomotive tools can be added here. Perhaps add a slacking pipe over the cab side made from fine wire insulation tube.

6.
OPERATION

I have advocated throughout this series that a model railway that is developed with regard to the whole picture rather than absolute scale fidelity is likely to be more rewarding. My interest in model railways is less an interest in the individual items of the railway but rather in this total picture - I am, I suppose, in effect trying to re-create in model form my memories, which are of the railway scene as a whole rather than the detail of, say, a particular tender. This is not, however, to say that accuracy is not important, as inaccuracy of detail will detract from the totality of the picture and the impression it leaves.

We have looked at a whole range of items that make up the impression we are trying to create, from planning through buildings and landscape to the locomotives and stock we are using. Surely in building up this impression we also have to look at how the trains are operated, their formations and, perhaps most importantly, how the trains will move around on our layout.

Perhaps my perspective on railway modelling comes from not really being a 'railway enthusiast' and never, dare I say, in my childhood a particularly keen trainspotter! I did, however, enjoy watching the trains, be it steaming through the local landscape or a '4F' shunting the local goods yard for hours on end.

The thing about all these railway movements is that they happened for a purpose, and conformed to rules and regulations and to the unwritten rules of circumstances. By the latter point I mean traffic requirements, availability of locomotives and rolling-stock and accepted practices of the area.

One of my fondest recollections is many years ago now, watching David Jenkinson's Garsdale Road layout at an exhibition. I stood among the crowd and was instantly back to watching the trains, although in a far more rural landscape than that of my childhood. The track layout, buildings and structures were pure Settle & Carlisle, the train formations typical of the

service run at the period that the model was representing and, just like on the real thing, I didn't know what was coming next - the fiddle yard was totally hidden from view. Just as on the real thing I knew when something was coming and in which direction by observing the signals. It created an impression from the total scene it represented and by its operation, which was typical of the piece of railway being modelled - not by the individual models.

Personally, therefore, I suppose that in viewing a model railway I want to be in that position of my youth, of 'watching the trains', where their operation is just as important as the stock and the buildings in creating the scene I want to watch.

I have discussed the *raison d'être* of the locomotives and stock and the services we are operating on Platt Lane in the appropriate sections earlier. Suffice here then just to add one or two comments.

In essence, with any modelling project we are trying to create an illusion of reality, and one of the easiest ways to shatter that illusion is to do something inappropriate. You would not for example encourage the use of the exceptions to normality, hence my choice of what some would regard as fairly dull, ordinary locos and stock. Yes, in all probability an '8F' might have hauled freight into Platt Lane and a 'Black Five' might have handled some traffic, particularly post-1959. However, the very ordinariness, if there is such a word, is an essential part of the illusion.

In Great Moor Street, from which we have drawn the inspiration for Platt Lane, it was common for there to be two push-pull sets in use, the Kenyon Junction one and, outside peak traffic hours, one to Manchester Exchange. Commonly, rather than find a separate rake of coaches, strengtheners were added to the two-coach push-pull sets and these, obviously no longer used as push-pull trains, operated peak-hour services. Former Midland Railway Bain 48-foot stock was used in the late '40s, often hauled by Fowler 2-6-2T No 58.

If we had two push-pull sets on Platt Lane they would be in all probability of similar vehicles and, on the model, a little boring. So I have still maintained the link with actuality in choosing the formation I described earlier.

There is also another good reason for the choice, that of space. Not only are we creating an illusion, but also most of us have little enough space in which to do it. Certainly there is no room on Platt Lane for five-coach trains!

However, one compromise would be to use a push-pull set as we are for the model equivalent of the Kenyon Junction service, but just add one coach as a strengthener for the peak-hour service as an alternative to our corridor set.

The point I want to make regarding these vehicles and trains is that in reality they travel several routes on their journeys and even in intense 'suburban' settings some time would pass before they would be seen again in the station. There was a diagram in late LMS/early BR days that started from Manchester London Road with a local to Crewe. The stock then spent 2½ days visiting places like Shrewsbury, Hereford, Stafford and Stoke before arriving back at Manchester London Road. The first point on operation, then, is not to have the same train shuttling in and out every few seconds. Remember that when your train departs it is going somewhere and will be gone for some time.

Perhaps one of the most common illusion-breakers is the speed at which trains are operated on model railways. On the Steam Age railway the speed of a train was determined by the location, type and traffic of the train. The majority of freight trains even in 1959 were made up of unfitted stock, and these infamous loose-coupled trains were slow, ponderous things, and their smaller brethren, the local pick-up freights and trip workings, were more akin to tortoise than hare! Passenger trains didn't fly round the curve and stop abruptly at the station; the train would have been slowed by the outer home signal and, if approaching sidings or a station, especially a terminus with a platform not completely clear, would halt completely prior to being allowed to proceed slowly.

There are certainly occasions on Platt Lane when light engine movements are called for. In the confines of a station light engines tend to give an air of bustle, but this should be represented carefully, not at express speeds but building from a slow start and stopping not too abruptly.

While on the subject of engine movements, when shunting steam locomotives did not undertake flying changes of direction. Reverse gear had to be selected either buy turning a large hand wheel in the case of screw reverse or moving a large lever in the case of lever reverse. Engines had to be stopped, albeit momentarily, prior to reversing. Many of the mechanical, operational and regulatory requirements took time to complete and required pauses before the next stage of the movement. For example, a locomotive backing on to a train would buffer up, the coupling would need to be hooked on - loco to coach or wagon - and adjusted and, if vacuum fitted, the vacuum brake connected. Before the train could move the vacuum had to be created and the brakes checked for pressure. Lamps had to be fitted to the loco and to the rear of the train. In unhooking from a train this happened in reverse and, of course, also took time. So don't race your train engine down to the train and send it out again without the appropriate pause.

On the subject of light engines and their use on Platt Lane, it will be necessary for trains to be taken from their arrival platform by pilot engine prior to either being positioned in another platform for departure or removal to the carriage sidings (alias the fiddle yard). The engine that brought in the train should then not be left at the end of the platform as it would be out of view of the signalman, which was against operating regulations. It would in reality follow its train out, at least into the vision of the signalman at the end of the platform where it might wait pending further instructions.

I could go on with various examples of real, essential railway practice rarely witnessed on models. Suffice to say that the steam railway was not the all-action, or rather constant-action, scene often assumed, and either of mechanical or regulatory necessity certain things had to happen causing pauses between movements and speeds of passage. I think that if nothing else the model railway operator needs to pause before and between movements, to think about what he is doing and not to rush anything.

While the real steam railway has gone, much of what we have just discussed can be witnessed on some of the excellent archive railway videos now available.

Epilogue: where do we go from here?

In these three volumes concerning the building of Platt Lane, we have looked at how one average model railway has been built in the hope that the philosophy behind it and the techniques used in its construction will be of interest. As I have said repeatedly, there is nothing special about Platt Lane or the techniques used to build it - it is an average, hopefully working model railway that we will take to some exhibitions.

No model railway is ever finished, and certainly Platt Lane isn't. It is always possible to continue adding detail, improving individual items, adding rolling-stock, improving operation or indeed adding extensions.

Clearly during the time taken to build and develop any model railway, standards improve, knowledge is gained and some of the things we were happy with at the beginning may now not seem to us to be as good as our latest models or fit in with the greater knowledge we have acquired. That is the nature of railway modelling - as the teacher said: 'Could do better'.

Platt Lane drew its inspiration from Bolton Great Moor Street, which had a life of 70 years or so and could possibly have survived even beyond our projected 1959. This gives possibilities for backdating or updating the model - although I guess a cut-back single platform, 'bus shelter', car park and supermarket wouldn't give such a good operating potential. Lines from Great Moor Street ran to a junction, and certainly any extension could represent that, giving either a reversing loop or double fiddle yard, both of which would take quite a considerable space.

I have in mind a rather more simple extension suitable for use at exhibitions or in the larger house I have promised myself when I win the lottery jackpot: a mere 8 feet or so in two 4-foot boards, one before the fiddle yard incorporating a couple of carriage sidings parallel to the main approaches, and a 4-foot extension on the platform, possibly incorporating a slight curve to enhance the visual presence of the layout.

Unless the fiddle yard was extended, train lengths would still be restricted by the length of the fiddle yard. Not that I would really want longer trains, but the longer platforms would also help to create the illusion of space. Nothing planned in detail yet - just a few ideas. . .

It would be interesting to hear from you via the publisher to see how you would envisage the layout developing. What about it?

And finally. . . If the front end of your loco isn't quite up to the standard you would have liked, or if that brake van just *won't* run smoothly - don't worry. Worse things happen on the prototype!

GLOSSARY OF ROLLING-STOCK TERMS

Beading
Moulding applied to cover joints in panelling or sheeting.

Bogie
A separate, self-contained and mobile arrangement allowing long vehicles, generally coaches, to move around corners. Bogies normally have four or six wheels, and a vehicle would generally have one bogie at either end. On locomotives a bogie carries weight, for example under a bunker; at the front of a locomotive the independent though controlled movement of a bogie guides the locomotive. A pony-truck is a single-axle two-wheel bogie.

Buffers
Telescopic, sprung plungers compressing to protect and cushion the impact between vehicles. Railway companies tended to develop their own style, which a long-lived vehicle might have replaced later in its life.

Compensation
A system to allow vertical motion of one or all axles on a vehicle or locomotive in response to variations in rail height.

Cantrail
The point at which coach sides and roof meet.

Connecting rod
The rod linking the cylinders and pistons to the driving wheels.

Coupling rod
The rod seen on virtually all steam locomotives and some diesel shunters connecting the wheels and transferring power from the driving wheel (driven by the connecting rod) to all driving wheels.

Couplings
There are four main types:
Three-link: A hook on the headstock has three chain links attached to it. The end of the chain is linked on to the hook of the vehicle to be coupled. These couplings are found on unfitted wagons and locomotives.
Instanter: These again have hooks and three links but the centre link has a T-shaped centre to allow it to be turned around so that the shorter cross-section forces the link to tighten the slack in the coupling. These couplings are used on fitted goods stock.
Screw: Again there is a hook from which the coupling is suspended, but this time it comprises two U-shaped links connected to a central threaded bar which has a 'tommy bar' to enable it to be turned to tighten any slack. These couplings are found on fitted vehicles, coaches and locomotives.
Buckeye: Although in use in the USA for many years, their use only became commonplace in the UK on coaches built from the mid-1960s. They enable automatic coupling and operate, as their name suggests, by 'clasping'.

Diagram Number
A number identifying a vehicle, derived from the railway's Diagram Book, which defined each type of vehicle built.

Drag-beam/drawbar
The transverse section beneath the cab footplate and tender front that carries the couplings between the two. 'Drawgear' also refers to the couplings including the parts usually hidden behind the headstocks.

Droplight
The opening window in a coach doors that drops down inside the door when opened.

Ejector
A system of valves often located outside the smokebox to enable a vacuum to be created for braking.

Footboard
A stepboard fixed to either the side of a coach bogie or along the length of the solebar.

Headstock
The end of the underframe on coaches and wagons carrying the buffers and drawgear.

Injector
A device that forces water into a locomotive boiler against the steam pressure.

Lining
The coloured lines drawn along locomotives and coaches adding relief to the main colour and often used, in the case of locomotives, to define the shape of a panel such as a cab or tank side.

Livery
The colour scheme of a particular vehicle usually determined by the corporate 'house style' of the owning company.

Lubricator
A usually mechanically operated device providing lubrication to key parts of the motion while the vehicle is moving. Often located on the footplate, the lubricator will have pipe runs to the parts its serves. Lubricators come in a variety of types but Wakefield and Silvertown are the most common.

Pick-up
The system of collecting current from the rail, usually via the wheels, to enable it to be fed to the motor to power a locomotive.

Rainstrips
Narrow strips applied to roofs, sometimes continuously, to prevent rainwater from dripping over doors and windows from the roof.

Sanding gear
A box containing dry sand and pipe runs to deliver sand to the rails adjacent to a locomotive's driving wheels to improve adhesion. Fitted to steam locomotives and first-generation diesels, but not, as BR has found to its cost, later generation units.

Solebar
The main longitudinal beam running the length of a coach or wagon between the headstocks.

Toplight
A small window separate from and above a main carriage window. The use of top-lights in certain coach designs resulted in them being known as 'Toplights'.

Truss-rods
An arrangement of steel section giving structural support and strength to a vehicle underframe.

Tumblehome
The inward curve of the lower part of a coach side giving the vehicle its profile.

Valve gear
The various rods and cranks operating the steam valves on a locomotive's cylinders and transmitting the power from the cylinders to the driving wheels. Valve gear many be inside or outside the main frames, and is often referred to as the 'motion'. Walschaerts gear is the most common outside type and is seen on both the larger Platt Lane locos.

Ventilators (Stones/Dewel)
Two similar patterns of ventilator used on LMS coaches. They were positioned above the windows and comprised a series of glass panes that swivelled together, like vertical louvres, to control ventilation.

Wagon brakes
All wagons have as a minimum a hand-brake, usually operated by a lever outside the solebar. On earlier vehicles the lever may be on one side only and may not operate on all the wheels. In a brake van the brakes are controlled from inside by the guard. Vehicles with handbrakes only are called 'unfitted'; those with additional continuous vacuum-operated brakes are 'fitted'. The latter are controlled from the locomotive, hence the need to have fitted vehicles behind the locomotive in a train composed of both types. Some unfitted vehicles contain the necessary piping to allow the vacuum brake to pass through them to adjacent fitted vehicles; these vehicles were referred to as 'piped'.

INDEX